# NEW TESTAMENT
# MYSTERIES

Let a man so account of us, as of the ministers of Christ, and stewards of the mysteries of God. Moreover, it is required in stewards, that a man be found faithful.

I Corinthians 4:1, 2

Arthur D. Jackson

New Testament Mysteries
by Arthur D. Jackson

First Printing
July, 1996

Copyright © 1996 Focus Publishing, Inc.
All Rights Reserved

*No part of this book may be reproduced by any*
*means without written consent of the publisher*
*except for brief quotes used in reviews written*
*specifically for use in a magazine or newspaper.*

All scripture references are from the King James Version of the Bible.

ISBN 1-885904-10X

PRINTED IN THE UNITED STATES OF AMERICA
BY
FOCUS PUBLISHING, INC.
1375 Washington Avenue South
Bemidji, Minnesota 56601

*This Book Is Dedicated*
*In Loving Memory of*

Rev. EARL MORGAN

Man of God, gentle instructor, good friend,
whose faithful ministry while serving on the faculty
of Multnomah School of the Bible in Portland, Oregon,
led me into the truths that comprise the bulk of this study.

# TABLE OF CONTENTS

| | | | |
|---|---|---|---|
| Introduction | | | i |
| The Mystery Age | | | iv |
| Schematic : | New Testament Mysteries - Figure 1 | | vii |
| Chapter I | The Mysteries of the Kingdom of Heaven | | 1 |
| | Definition of the Kingdom of Heaven | | 2 |
| | Outline of the Kingdom of Heaven - Figure 2 | | 5 |
| Chapter II | The Mysteries of Matthew 13 | | 7 |
| | 1) The Sower | Matt. 13:3-9 | 7 |
| | 2) The Tares | Matt. 13:24-30 | 13 |
| | Illus. of Tares - Figure 3 | | 18 |
| | 3) The Mustard Seed | Matt. 13:31-32 | 19 |
| | 4) The Leaven | Matt. 13:33 | 20 |
| | 5) The Treasure | Matt. 13:44 | 22 |
| | 6) The Pearl | Matt. 13:45-46 | 23 |
| | 7) The Dragnet | Matt. 13:47-50 | 26 |
| | The Relationship of the Kingdoms - Figure 4 | | 27 |
| Chapter III | The Mysteries of the Kingdom of God | | 29 |
| Chapter IV | The Mystery of the Wisdom of God | | 35 |
| Chapter V | The Mystery of the Gospel | | 43 |
| Chapter VI | The Mystery of His Will | | 55 |
| | Adoption | | 61 |
| | Predestination | | 67 |
| Chapter VII | The Mystery of The Faith | | 71 |
| Chapter VIII | The Mystery of the In-Living Christ | | 77 |
| | The Benefits of Salvation - Figure 5 | | 81 |

| | | | |
|---|---|---|---|
| Chapter IX | The Mystery of Godliness | | 83 |
| Chapter X | The Mystery of Iniquity | | 89 |
| Chapter XI | The Mystery of the Church | | 95 |
| | 1) Shepherd and Sheep | | 100 |
| | 2) Vine and Branches | | 102 |
| | 3) Head and Members | | 104 |
| | 4) Cornerstone and Living Stones | | 108 |
| | 5) Last Adam and New Creation | | 113 |
| | 6) Bridegroom and Bride | | 117 |
| | 7) High Priest and a Royal Priesthood | | 122 |
| |    a) Qualifications for the priesthood | | 122 |
| |    b) Work of a priest | | 125 |
| |    c) Atonement | | 126 |
| |    d) Our High Priest | | 127 |
| |    e) Secure in Christ | | 128 |
| | INTERCESSOR(S) | | 131 |
| | A KINGDOM OF PRIESTS | | 133 |
| Chapter XII | The Mystery of the Change (physically: before the rapture) | | 135 |
| Chapter XIII | The Mystery of Israel's Blindness | | 141 |
| Chapter XIV | The Mystery of the Seven Stars | | 147 |
| | 1) Ephesus | Rev. 2:1-7 | 148 |
| | 2) Smyrna | Rev. 2:8-11 | 150 |
| | 3) Pergamos | Rev. 2:12-17 | 151 |
| | 4) Thyatira | Rev. 2:18-29 | 153 |
| | 5) Sardis | Rev. 3:1-6 | 155 |
| | 6) Philadelphia | Rev. 3:7-13 | 156 |
| | 7) Laodicea | Rev. 3:14-19 | 157 |
| Chapter XV | Mystery Babylon | | 159 |
| Chapter XVI | The Mystery of God is Finished | | 165 |

# INTRODUCTION

In my capacity as a Bible teacher and a college instructor I have found a real lack of material available for a course text book dealing with the study of the subject of New Testament mysteries. I have, in teaching on this topic, discovered that it has met with an excellent reception by students; in addition, it is a fascinating subject on its own merits and one worthy of further investigation. It is due to the scant amount of written information on this matter that I have been encouraged to make an attempt to help fill the void with some material --- the product of many years of teaching and reflection --- that I trust will prove instructive.

The word "mystery" occurs twenty seven times in the authorized version of the New Testament. It is a translation of the Greek word "musterion," which is a derivative of "muo" which means "to shut the mouth," connoting "silence". A common word used today that has the same root source is the word moustache; hair on the upper lip. The Greek word "mystax" which means upper lip and also the word "mastax" translated mouth or jaw, are both of this same family. Thus it is said that when we eat a meal we masticate our food before swallowing. In this light, it can be concluded that the word mystery as used in the New Testament would literally mean a closed-mouth silence.

The modern dictionary meaning of the word "mystery" is twofold: 1) something which is unintelligible, incomprehensive, baffling, or uncanny and 2) something which may be known but only by the initiated. The ancient meaning is connected with the ancient cults of Babylon and of Rome and it follows the sense of the second meaning listed above. The heathen religious ceremonies practiced by these cults consisted of rites considered sacred and observed in strictest secrecy. Those who were initiated into the order were known as the "perfected" and were then exposed to these rites.

The New Testament and biblical definition of a "mystery" is best seen in the Apostle Paul's letter to the Church in Ephesus when he wrote,

*"That which in other ages was <u>not made known</u> unto the sons of men, as it is now revealed unto his holy apostles and prophets by the Spirit." (Eph. 3:5).*

This is not an isolated text but is very much reinforced by several other Scripture passages such as the one found in the last chapter of the letter to the church at Rome.

*"Now to him that is of power to establish you according to my gospel, and the preaching of Jesus Christ, according to the revelation of the MYSTERY, which was <u>kept secret</u> since the world began, but <u>NOW</u> is made manifest, and by the scriptures of the prophets according to the commandment of the everlasting God, made known to all nations for the obedience of faith." (Ro. 16:25-26).*

The Holy Spirit repeats this truth the third time for even greater emphasis when He has Paul explain in the letter to the Colossians,

*"Even the MYSTERY which has been <u>hidden</u> from ages and from generations, but <u>NOW</u> is made manifest to his saints, to whom God would make known what is the riches of the glory of this MYSTERY among the Gentiles, which is Christ in you, the hope of glory." (Col. 1:26-27).*

The words of the old cliche, "We should make much of that which God makes much of," is fitting in this matter: when God repeats a truth three times there has to be a reason for it, a very good reason.

We may conclude, then, that the "mysteries" spoken of in the New Testament embody those truths which in the ages prior to Pentecost were kept in silence, but in the church age are made accessible and the potential common knowledge of all believers. They are not special truths for an elite group but every believer is privileged to understand

and possess the knowledge of these mysteries. In fact each and every believer has a definite responsibility before God to both know and teach these truths. As the Apostle Paul wrote:

*"Let a man so account of us, as of the ministers of Christ, and stewards of the mysteries of God. Moreover, it is required in stewards, that a man be found faithful." (I Cor. 4:1-2).*

The word "stewards" as used in these verses is very intriguing and worthy of some elucidation. The use of such easily available sources as encyclopedias, dictionaries, concordances, etc. can be of extensive value in this type of study to give depth and insight to words used in the Scriptures. Strong's Exhaustive Concordance gives this term as the translation of the Greek word "oikonomia" as the Apostle Paul used the word in First Corinthians. Further study shows that "oikonomia" occurs three times in Luke's gospel chapter sixteen, and each time it is rendered "stewardship." (Lk. 16:2,3,4). On four other occasions in the New Testament this word is translated "dispensation." (I Cor. 9:17; Eph. 1:10,3:2; Col. 1:25). The English word "economy" is derived from this Greek word and means "to manage." One dictionary definition of "economy" is "frugal management of money, materials, resources, and the like; freedom from extravagance; thrift."

The word "dispense" may be easily recognized at the core of the larger word "dispensation." To "dispense" means to administer, to distribute or deal out in portions. The term "stewardship" comes from the old German "stigweard" which may be translated literally as "housewarden." A housewarden, according to the dictionary is an "officer or employee in a large family, estate, etc. to manage the domestic concerns, supervise servants, collect rents, keep accounts, etc." "The steward would be an administrator, supervisor, manager in a closed economy."

In this light the importance and magnitude of what the Apostle Paul has written in I Cor. 4:1-2 concerning every believer being a steward or having a stewardship is borne out. Each Christian has a responsibility to read and learn of the different New Testament Mysteries in such a way as to be able to relay them on to others.

# THE MYSTERY AGE

The church age is best known by its more popular name, the "age of grace." A third name and one which perhaps is the most appropriate of all is the "mystery age" and will be the one used in this study. This mystery age began on the day of Pentecost (recorded in Acts chapter two) and will continue until the day when the Church is raptured (caught up) to meet the Lord in the air. The Church itself is a New Testament mystery since it is entirely unknown and unrevealed in Old Testament scriptures. It is the Church, the body of which Christ is the head, that is the basic theme around which all the other mysteries revolve. As shown in figure #1, the individual mysteries lead toward the Church or surround it in a revealing fashion and collectively expose this culminating work of God to the minds and understanding of inquiring persons who desire to know of God and His plans for this age. The New Testament mysteries reveal the Church in its purpose, composition, character, and history, in its relationship to Christ and much other pertinent data. All that may be known of the True Church, the corporate body of Christ, is found in the messages that the New Testament mysteries provide. All of the New Testament mysteries are germane and applicable in this age in which we now live.

Fifteen New Testament mysteries are listed in the order they occur in scripture. Note that the first two are found in the Gospels and the last two are located in the Book of Revelation recorded by the Apostle John. The first two mysteries actually locate the Church in reference to other parts of God's overall program. I wish to draw a distinction between the kingdom of heaven and the kingdom of God (and will explain this below), but the Church will be seen as comprising a part of both of these kingdoms, though relating somewhat differently to each. The Church is composed only of those "born again" members of all the generations of this present mystery age; generations both past and present since Christ. Because of their "born again" experience they are referred to as the good seed or as wheat. The Kingdom of Heaven is concerned only with the presently living generation, and it embraces both wheat and tares. For this reason the Kingdom of Heaven in any given generation may be regarded as much larger than the True Church of the same period of time. The Church is seen also to be part of the Kingdom of God, but this kingdom is far greater in scope than the Church. The Kingdom of God is essentially a spiritual kingdom and it contains all creatures of all time who are willing subjects of God's rule. Thus the Kingdom of God includes the holy angels, the Old Testament saints, and those redeemed persons who comprise the Church.

It is to be concluded that every believer of this mystery age is a member of three different divinely ordained economies; first, he is a member of the Church; second, he is a member of the Kingdom of Heaven in its mystery form and here on earth; and third, he is a member of the spiritual and eternal Kingdom of God. The literal Kingdom of Heaven has been postponed until the return of its King after the mystery age is complete. God's main thrust and purpose in this present age is the "calling out" of the Church. This Church, which is to be "The Bride of Christ," will sit by His side and rule with Him all during the next age which is known as the millennium, or the literal realization of Kingdom of Heaven.

The final two mysteries, both found in the book of Revelation, give the course and the history of the True Church throughout this age which is then followed by the course and destruction of the false church which remains on earth after the True Church is removed. The remaining eleven mysteries are from the epistles and the pen of the Apostle Paul who, according to Ephesians chapter three received them by direct revelation from God (Eph. 3:3-4).

| | |
|---|---:|
| 1) The Mysteries of the Kingdom of Heaven | Matt. 13 |
| 2) The Mysteries of the Kingdom of God | Mk. 4:11; Lk. 8:10 |
| 3) The Mystery of Israel's Blindness | Ro. 11:25 |
| 4) The Mystery of the Wisdom of God | I Cor. 2:7; Col. 2:2 |
| 5) The Mystery of the Change  (at the Rapture) | I Cor. 15:51 |
| 6) The Mystery of His Will | Eph. 1:9 |

| | |
|---|---|
| 7) The Mystery of Christ (the Church) | Eph. 3:3-9 |
| 8) The Mystery of the Church (the Bride) | Eph. 5:32 |
| 9) The Mystery of the Gospel | Eph. 6:19 |
| 10) The Mystery of the Inliving Christ | Col. 1:26 |
| 11) The Mystery of Iniquity | II Thess. 2:7 |
| 12) The Mystery of Faith | I Tim. 3:9 |
| 13) The Mystery of Godliness | I Tim. 3:16 |
| 14) The Mystery of the Seven Stars | Rev. 1:20 |
| 15) Mystery Babylon | Rev. 17:5-7 |

These mysteries comprise the bulk of church truth and are separate from, though complementary to, Old Testament teaching. In each case the New Testament use of the word "mystery" indicates a new work of God that had been previously unrevealed, totally unknown and untaught in the Old Testament.

The two mysteries at the top of the list are each spoken of in the plural form as "mysteries" because they are respectively made up of a number of different truths or ideas expressed in multiple parables. The mysteries surrounding the Kingdom of Heaven are exposed to the reader through seven different parables, each one revealing some new and diverse truth concerning that subject. There are three parables associated with the truth relating to the mysteries of the Kingdom of God. If each of these parables is treated as revealing a separate mystery as some Bible scholars and teachers do, then the list would add up to twenty-three instead of fifteen.

# *New Testament Mysteries*
By: Art Jackson

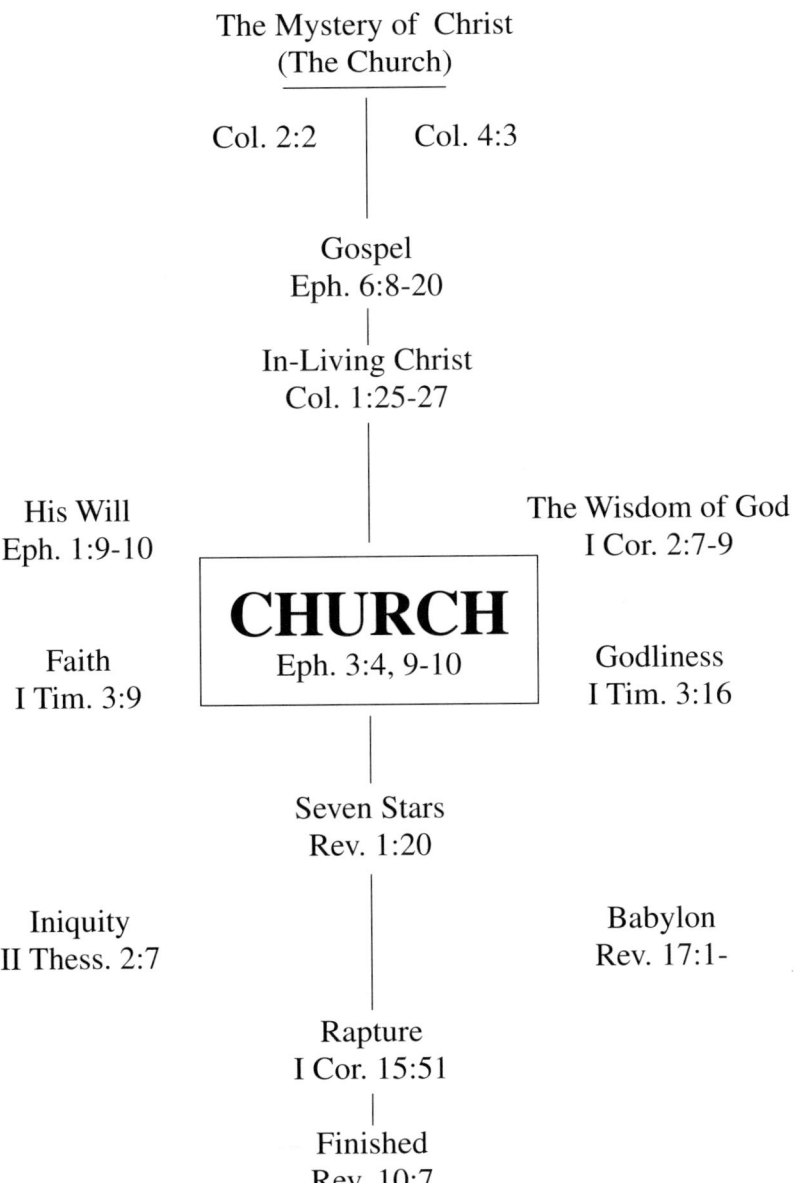

Figure #1

## Chapter I
## The MYSTERIES of the Kingdom of Heaven

The Kingdom of Heaven is not the Church. The mysteries of the Kingdom of Heaven are given to reveal the relationship that does exist between this kingdom and the Church and show that each is a separate and distinct entity.

We will begin this study with the first use of the word "mystery" as it is used in the New Testament. This first occurrence is found in Matthew's gospel, in the eleventh verse of the thirteenth chapter, where we read, "It is given unto you to know the mysteries of the Kingdom of Heaven." In the New Testament, Matthew alone speaks of the "mysteries of the kingdom of heaven." In truth, the expression "kingdom of heaven" is unique to the first gospel which often times is referred to as the Jewish gospel. The three following gospels, Mark, Luke, and John, speak of the Kingdom of God and of the "mysteries of the kingdom of God".

This passage in Matthew thirteen does not say that the Kingdom of Heaven is the mystery, and indeed it cannot be because the Kingdom of Heaven is spoken of and taught about in the Old Testament. According to the definition of a New Testament Mystery, it had to consist of a truth that had been maintained in absolute silence all during prior ages. What Matthew thirteen is saying is there are many things about the Kingdom of Heaven that were previously unrevealed but are now being taught to the church. The truth contained in the seven parables of Matthew thirteen gives the church a view of the Kingdom of Heaven never before seen by men.

# THE KINGDOM OF HEAVEN

Before proceeding with the study of the mysteries, it would be profitable to define the subject to which this group of mysteries pertain, namely, the Kingdom of Heaven. There is a substantial amount of uncertainty, misinformation, and even outright dispute regarding this subject. What is the Kingdom of Heaven? Where is it? and When is it? These are some of the questions that need to be answered before continuing on with the broader study.

In my old school days I recall that one of the methods of learning was to present a theory and then proceed to demonstrate that proposed theory to be correct. This proved to be a very acceptable method of education and I will attempt to use it now in furthering this study of the Kingdom of Heaven. First the theory: The Kingdom of Heaven is not a kingdom IN heaven, but it is heaven's rule here on earth. This kingdom is set up and established by God; with His Son, Jesus, The Christ, as the One who sits on the throne — David's throne — on Mount Zion in Jerusalem. It is a kingdom consisting of living, breathing human beings with all the rights and privileges of citizens of any other earthly kingdom. The citizens of the Kingdom of Heaven can own property, be taxed, vote, travel, marry, reproduce, etc. This necessarily limits the Kingdom of Heaven at any given moment to the then living generation.

The name "kingdom of heaven" originated from the word of prophecy outlined in the book of Daniel where we read,

> "And in the days of these kings shall the God of heaven set up a kingdom, which shall never be destroyed -- and it shall stand forever." (Dan. 2:44).

As shall be shown, this is speaking of a literal government here on earth not unlike any other government under which men live and thrive. The preceding verses of Daniel, chapter two, tell of a vision a king had of a great image or idol. During the interpretation of this vision, the great image is revealed to picture the course of gentile world government or gentile world supremacy. Gentile world supremacy — what a phrase for men to meditate upon and conjure up pictures and scenes from the past. When written by Daniel, all these things were prophetic and future, but in their time they became real and literal even though today they are mostly historical. The image is said to have a head of gold which is stated to represent the Babylonian empire and its great king Nebuchadnezzar. The breast and arms of the image were made of silver which is said to represent the empire of the Medes and Persians. This was followed by the belly and thighs made of bronze, picturing the Greek empire that arose under Alexander the Great. The description of the image was then completed by disclosing the legs made of iron and the feet made of iron mixed with clay which speak of the Roman empire and the final gentile world government which is yet future and thus is unfulfilled prophecy at the time of this writing.

Rome, in its yet future form, will be partly strong and partly weak; this is what is intimated in the statement that the toes were a mixture of iron and clay. The ten toes representing the final form of the Roman empire show that empire to be a confederation of ten kings. To complete the picture, Daniel 2:34 further prophesies that a stone (Christ) "cut out without hands," strikes the image on the feet and the whole image is destroyed. The stone then becomes a great mountain filling the whole earth. In the language of prophesy, a mountain often speaks of the seat of government (See Isa. 2:2-3). This reference would then mean the government the Lord establishes would be world wide. This mountain filling the whole earth is none other than the kingdom of heaven. At His second coming, Jesus the Christ, will put an end to all gentile government. He will set up His own government which will be world wide, and men know His rule as the Millennial Kingdom. This will be the literal Kingdom of Heaven.

This of course is highly pictorial language. Secular history reveals that much of this has in fact come to pass. The four gentile world powers, Babylon, Media/Persia, Greece, and Rome, are a matter of historical record and they did occur in the order given. The four empires were real, political, physical entities here on earth, and there is no reason to believe the fifth government, the one to be set up by the God of heaven, will be any less so. This fifth kingdom, the kingdom of heaven, is yet future and will not be seen in its real form until the second coming of Jesus Christ who will be its King and Chief Administrator. When it is set up and becomes an actuality, it will be known as the Millennial

Kingdom and is the "kingdom of Heaven" in that kingdom's literal form and existence. It will be heaven's reign on the earth and its subjects will be real, living, breathing human beings. Its King will be seated on David's throne in its capital city Jerusalem.

In the first book of the Bible, Gen. 13:14-15, the LORD speaks to a man named Abram and gives to him by word of promise, all the land of Canaan for an <u>EVERLASTING</u> possession, Gen. 17:8. This promise made by God is earthly in its outlook with very well known real estate in view, having very real boundaries. This man Abram, who later became Abraham, was the progenitor of the Jewish people or Jewish race. It was to another Jewish man, David, to whom God also spoke and enlarged the original promise. The Scriptures speak in II Samuel 7:12-21 that to the initial pledge of land would now be added the promise of a throne, a king, and a kingdom that would endure <u>FOREVER</u>. Note carefully that all that is being spoken of is very earthly; the land is Palestine, the throne is Jewish, the king is Davidic, and the capital is Jerusalem.

As the New Testament opens, the very first verse, Matthew 1:1, reads that Jesus Christ is the son of David, the son of Abraham thus immediately linking Him with the promises given centuries before. Furthermore, the very first public statement made concerning Jesus was in the form of a question asked by those who were seeking Him; "Where is he that is born king of the Jews?" (Matt. 2:2) As His earthly ministry began the announcement was proclaimed, "the Kingdom of heaven is at hand." (Matt. 4:17) The kingdom could have been set up promptly at that time, for the King was present in the person of Jesus. It is also a matter of record that the last public statement made concerning Him was in a written note fastened above His head as He hung on the cross and died. The note read, "This is Jesus, the king of the Jews" (Matt. 27:37). Thus, it is seen that the Jews rejected Jesus as their <u>king</u>; in effect, they said "we will not have this man reign over us." John's gospel declares, "He came unto his own, and his own received him not" (Jn. 1:11).

Because the <u>king</u> was rejected, the kingdom was postponed to a future date and God began a new and different program among men. He is now calling out a body of believers that is given the name "the Church," and as He does this, mankind is living in and through the "mystery Age". Entrance into the "kingdom of heaven in its mystery form" as it exists today in this the church age, is offered to all men. Here we have used the two terms "Kingdom of Heaven" and "The Church" in the same sentence but wish to underscore the fact they are two vastly different entities. In the present age, "The Church" is of principal importance and is the primary object of God's attention and effort. He is calling out a body of believers that will be the "Bride" of His Son. The "Kingdom of Heaven" does exist in this mystery age but it does so with an absent and unseen king. After "The Church" is taken up from earth and upon the return of the Lord, the rightful king, the Kingdom of Heaven will again regain significant importance and will come into its own as an actuality. The kingdom of heaven will reach its full manifestation upon the return of its absent king with the resulting installation of the millennial reign of Christ over the earth.

## *OUTLINE: THE KINGDOM OF HEAVEN*

"The term Kingdom of Heaven is fittingly applied to God's rule in the earth --- it is heaven's rule on the earth --- and is restricted in respect to time, to limited periods, and well defined situations." *L. S. Chafer*

Definition   Dan.2:44
    Heaven's rule on earth --- earthly.

I.    The Kingdom Promised. Num. 24:7
    A.    The Abrahamic Covenant
        Gen. 12:1 - 3; 13:14 - 17; 15:4 - 7; 17:1 - 8
        1. A land forever.   13:15
        2. A people or seed forever.   17:7 - 8

    B.    The Davidic Covenant
        II Sam. 7:12 - 21; 28 - 29; Jn. 7:42

1. A throne forever.
2. A king forever.
3. A kingdom forever.

II. The Kingdom in Prophecy
Isa . 9:6 - 7;  11:1 - 5    Jer. 23:5 - 6; 33:17; 21 - 22
Ezek. 37:21 - 28    Dan. 7:13 - 14
Hosea 3:4 - 5

III. The King Appears
Matt. 1:1;  2:2    Lk. 1:31 - 32,    Acts 2:25 - 31

IV. The Kingdom Offered
Matt. 3:1 - 2;  4:17;  10:5 - 7

V. The Kingdom Rejected
Acts 1:5 - 7    Jn. 1:11
Matt. 26:63 - 66; 27:1 - 2, 11, 37

VI. The Kingdom in Mystery Form
Matt. 13:

VII. The Kingdom Established
Matt. 25:31 - 34    Acts 15:16 - 18
Rev. 19:11 - 20:6    Psa. 2:1 - 9,  Isa. 63:1 - 6
II Thess. 1:7 - 9

A. With a rod
Isa. 11:4; 25:2 - 5; 30:29   Micah 5:5

figure #2

*Chapter II*

# THE MYSTERIES OF MATTHEW 13
# THE SOWER

*"Behold, a sower went forth to sow; And when he sowed, some of the seeds fell by the wayside, and the fowls came and devoured them. Some fell upon stony places, where they had not much earth; and forthwith they sprang up, because they had no deepness of earth. And when the sun was up, they were scorched; and because they had no root, they withered away. And some fell among thorns; and the thorns sprang up, and choked them. But other seeds fell into good ground, and brought forth fruit, some an hundredfold, some sixtyfold, some thirtyfold." (Matt. 13:3-8).*

*"Hear, therefore, the parable of the sower. When any one heareth the word of the kingdom, and understandeth it not, then cometh the wicked one, and catcheth away that which was sown in his heart. This is he which received seed by the wayside. But he that received the seed in stony places, the same is he that heareth the word, and immediately with joy receiveth it; Yet hath he not root in himself, but endureth for a while; for when tribulation or persecution ariseth because of the word, immediately he is offended. He also that received seed among the thorns is he that heareth the word; and the care of this age, and the deceitfulness of riches, choke the word, and he becometh unfruitful. But he that received seed in the good ground is he that heareth the word, and understandeth it, who also beareth fruit, and bringeth forth, some an hundredfold some sixty, some thirty." (Matt. 13:18-23).*

The first parable of this singular chapter, that of the "sower" found in verses 3 to 8 and 18 to 23, tells how men become citizens of the kingdom of heaven in its mystery form. There are at least two requirements for admission to this kingdom. 1) The necessity to hear the Word of God as it proclaims Christ to be the rightful ruler or king in the affairs of men and 2) the willingness on the part of men to accede to that claim and to some extent accept or at least profess to accept Him in that role in the individual life. The word profess is used here in a significant way because that is all that is required in the sight of men for entrance into the kingdom of heaven. To a large extent men are gauged by other men by what they say. The Bible puts it this way, "-- for the LORD seeth not as man seeth, for man looketh on the outward appearance, but the LORD looketh on the heart." (I Sam. 16:7b). The Apostle Paul showed concern over this same issue when he wrote his second letter to the church in Corinth and told the saints there:

*"Do ye look on things after the outward appearance? If any man trust to himself that he is Christ's, let him of himself think this again,— For not he that commendeth himself is approved, but whom the Lord commendeth." (II Cor. 10:7a, 18).*

The western nations are often spoken of as being "Christian Nations" and many citizens of those countries feel insulted, or at the very least become highly indignant indeed, if they are asked the question "are you a Christian?" The general belief is that they are "Christian" just because of where they were born or perhaps they think of it as an inherited condition, being an integral part of their citizenship. They would seldom admit to being pagan or ungodly. This <u>profession</u> of being "Christian", i.e. (being a believer in Christ), is the criterion for entrance into the Kingdom of Heaven.

Jesus explained His use of parables in this extraordinary method of teaching by saying "it is given unto you to <u>**KNOW**</u> the mysteries of the kingdom of heaven--" (Matt. 13:11). He then proceeds to tell a series of seven parables of which He gives a detailed explanation or interpretation of the first two. The interpretation of these two is the key for understanding the message given in all seven. As the story develops in the parable of the sower, Jesus informs His listeners that there are four different types of soil upon which the seed falls. These four different soils really represent four types of heart attitude of those people who hear the Word of God, the Bible. It is very important at this point to recognize the fact that all four "hear" and they all hear the same thing, the word of the kingdom. The first hearer can be dealt with rather quickly for it speaks of him as one that gives no reception or credence to the Word at all. This speaks of that individual who believes the Bible to be just a collection of myths or folk lore. He considers the Bible as being out of date, medieval, and thus of no relevance to this modern day and its problems. The Scriptures are brushed aside as having no value in this so called age of enlightenment. The remaining three hearers require a little more thoughtful perusal.

Luke is one of the writers who wrote on the subject of the kingdom of God; and in doing so he also discusses the topic of which we are engaged in, namely, the parable of the sower. As we shall discover later in the overall study of the "mysteries" one of the requirements for entrance into the kingdom of God is a new birth. (Jn. 3:3). To be "born again" means to have a new birth experience, which in turn means that the Word of God has more than a superficial impact on ones heart and life. When one makes a decision for God based on heart knowledge, then the promise of God is that the Holy Spirit will enter that heart and take up residence there. This is speaking of much more than a simple head knowledge of God's salvation, but rather it means the word of God has been put to the test of experience and found to be true. The very fact that it is stated these men turned away from the holy commandments is sufficient proof their heart was not committed to the truth of the word. While dealing with the parable of the sower, Luke inserts some startling information when addressing the subject of the good seed falling on rocky ground. He says, "They on the rock are they who, when they hear, receive the word with joy; and these have no root, who for awhile believe, and in time of testing fall away" (Lk. 8:13).

These people are said to "receive the word" and "for awhile believe." This would appear to be a classical illustration of intellectual belief. They have a head knowledge of the word but never let it get to the heart. The Word of God never becomes a major issue of the heart with them and the instruction the Bible gives is that men should "keep thy heart with all diligence; for out of it are the issues of life". (Pro. 4:23). In the New Testament, those who have life in Christ are given words of assurance and comfort when the Spirit says, "And the peace of God, which passeth all understanding, shall keep your hearts and minds through Jesus Christ." (Phil. 4:7) Here again the Scriptures give ample indication that the heart (emotions and affections) and the mind (intellect) are two separate entities but are required to be in absolute harmony when touching on the subject of salvation. The author James words it this way, "What doth it profit, my brethern, though a man say he hath faith, (belief) and have not works? (confession and actions) Can that faith save him? – Even so faith, if it hath not works, is dead, being alone." (James 2:14-17) The writer of the book of Hebrews adds his bit of evidence to the body of truth when he inscribes "Today if ye will hear his voice, harden not your hearts." (Heb. 4:7). This advice dovetails beautifully with the words of the Psalmist who wrote centuries earlier, "With my whole heart have I sought thee; oh, let me not wander from thy commandments. Thy word have I hidden in mine heart, that I might not sin against thee." (Psa. 119:10-11).

The parable of the Sower is dealing with the subject of belief and this word is defined as "acceptance of the truth; mental conviction; to have confidence; place ones trust; etc.". There can be many levels or degrees of belief and they will run the full gamut from near skepticism to outright dogmatism. Real danger may dwell with those who take stands or positions near either extreme of the expressed range of belief. The teaching from Matthew thirteen opens this aspect of truth for our thoughtful inspection.

The Bible gives some exacting instruction to those who are honestly seeking to know the truth. In the book of First Corinthians, it is stated: "Now we (believers) have received, not the spirit of the world, but the Spirit who is from God, that we might know the things freely given to us by God, which things we also speak not in words taught by human wisdom, but in those taught by the Spirit, combining spiritual thoughts with spiritual words." (I Cor. 2:12-13) NASB.

## Chapter 2

The parable of the Sower, while dealing with the subject of belief, zeros in on a belief whose end result is fruit bearing. One of the main Biblical references to fruit bearing is found in John's gospel chapter fifteen:

> *"I am the true vine,— Abide in Me, and I in you. As the branch cannot bear fruit of itself, except it abide in the vine no more can ye, except ye abide in Me. I am the vine, ye are the branches. He that abideth in Me, and I in him, the same bringeth forth much fruit; for without Me ye can do nothing. If a man abide not in Me, he is cast forth as a branch, and is withered; and men gather them, and cast them into the fire, and they are burned." (Jn. 15:1a, 4-6)*

Combining the truth given in the narrative of the vine and branches with that of the parable of the Sower a profound picture of truth begins to emerge. Not all men who profess to follow Christ are true believers in that they possess Him whole-heartedly or as the Scriptures say, they abide in Him. Some adhere to Christianity for social stature but their belief in the things of Christ is not top priority in their thinking or planning. For some, business success comes first, all else is secondary. If anything, including religion and/or ethics, gets in the way or becomes a hindrance to a promotion, a sale, or a bonus, it is jettisoned very quickly and easily. Modern business practices as well as modern social standards are readily accepted even though they may be unethical, amoral, and barely legal. The Apostle Peter wrote some sage advice concerning men of this nature.

> *"For if, after they have escaped the pollutions of the world through the knowledge of the Lord and Savior, Jesus Christ, they are again entangled in it, and overcome, the latter end is worse with them than the beginning. For it had been better for them not to have known the way of righteousness than, after they have known it, to turn from the holy commandment delivered unto them." (II Pet. 2:20-21.)*

These men had certain knowledge, head knowledge, of the truth. They were intellectually persuaded that what they had heard or read was true but due to existing circumstances, whether it be work, or friends, or social standing, or even politics, they turned away and would not incorporate it into their way of life. Now these things in themselves are not bad; but good. Work is good, friends are good, a social life is good, yes, even politicizing is good. But when a good thing comes first in life, first before God, it is wrong; it immediately becomes a stumbling block and a snare. These good things are absolutely essential in a working, successful society and God intended it to be that way. A man without family, without work, without friends, or without a social life is a troubled man, lonely, frustrated, and fertile ground for abject despair.

Jesus said "I am the vine, ye are the branches." It does not require a person to be a trained horticulturist to recognize the fact that the lower part of the vine contains the root, and the branches grow out from the upper end of the vine. The branches do not grow roots, but if they lack a vital connection with the vine, they will not receive the life-giving energy that comes up from the root through the vine. A branch that is without an essential union with the vine has no prospects of bearing fruit. It is possible to tie apples or oranges or any other type of fruit to the branches of a tree and for a short duration make it look good but over an extended period of time the deception will become apparent to any and all observers. Some branches may have a plethora of leaves and look very good and healthy, but if there is no fruit hidden among all the greenery the tree is of little value.

In the parable of the Sower, the second illustration reveals seed that falls on rocky ground and because of lack of soil has no root. The third illustration describes seed that falls among thorns and weeds and is soon choked and in this condition bears no fruit. The phrase, "the deceitfulness of riches" used in Matthew 13:22, is a phrase that brings various different mental pictures to mind. We are living in an age when success is too often judged on the basis of wealth. The entertainment business, including pro-sports, is a top illustration of this point. Many so called stars seem to have as their single objective the signing of the most lucrative contract. Second best does not count; the drive is always for first place. This singleness of mind leaves little place for godly living. "Christians" are not exempt from this error, and as the parable would have us know, good works are choked out and no godly fruit is produced. No root and no fruit; a tragic description of a majority who hear the gospel of salvation and even though they make a profession of accepting Christ, they are only play acting.

The fourth illustration speaks of seed that falls on good ground and produces fruit in various amounts of abundance. This illustration reveals the true believers; those who collectively make up the true Church, the body of Christ. It must be emphasized, there is a vast difference between the Kingdom of Heaven and the Church. The Kingdom of Heaven includes all those who simply <u>profess</u> to know or to follow Christ; the Church consists of all who <u>possess</u> Him. To possess Christ is to "abide" in the vine. This is the position of every believer who is born of the Spirit. It would be well to say that while every member of the church is a citizen of the Kingdom of Heaven, NOT every citizen of the Kingdom of Heaven is a member of the Church.

## THE PARABLE OF THE TARES PERTAINING TO TRUTH AND ERROR

*"Another parable put he forth unto them saying, The kingdom of heaven is likened unto a man who sowed good seed in his field; But, while men slept, his enemy came and sowed tares among the wheat, and went his way. But when the blade was sprung up, and brought forth fruit, then appeared the tares also. So the servants of the householder came and said unto him, Sir, didst not thou sow good seed in thy field? From where, then, hath it tares? He said unto them, An enemy hath done this. The servants said unto him, Wilt thou, then, that we go and gather them up? But he said, Nay; lest while ye gather up the tares, ye root up also the wheat with them. Let both grow together until the harvest; and in the time of harvest I will say to the reapers, Gather together first the tares, and bind them in bundles to burn them, but gather the wheat into my barn." (Matt. 13:18-30)*

*"His disciples came unto him saying, Explain unto us the parable of the tares of the field. He answered and said unto them, He that soweth the good seed is the Son of man; The field is the world; the good seed are the children of the kingdom, but the*

*tares are the children of the wicked one; The enemy that sowed them is the devil; the harvest is the end of the age; and the reapers are the angels. As, therefore, the tares are gathered and burned in the fire, so shall it be in the end of this age. The Son of man shall send forth his angels, and they shall gather out of his kingdom all things that offend, and them who do iniquity, And shall cast them into a furnace of fire; --."*
(Matt. 13:36-42).

The second parable, when coupled with the truth given in the first one, exhibits an emerging picture of the Kingdom of Heaven. A tare is a worthless grass or weed that in its early immature stage can hardly be distinguished from growing wheat. The two look so much alike in this immature period of growth they can only be identified with great care and much difficulty. The first parable taught that among believers there were those who had no root and yet others that bore no fruit. The Scriptures teach that "He is the vine, we are the branches" (Jn. 15:5) and it is a sure thing that any branch not attached to the vine has neither root nor fruit. At the best, these can only be called imitation believers and as the second parable indicates, they would certainly qualify as tares. The parable teaches that an enemy, during the night, sowed tares in the same field where the wheat was growing. While imparting this bit of information, the parable goes on to say that this impropriety is being carried on secretly and it is satanic in its origin. Satan's activity takes place at a time and in a manner in which most believers are caught almost totally oblivious. The parable says the tares were sown in the dark, "while men slept." Satan loves darkness and can't stand the light, for it exposes his evil activities.

Most false doctrine is sown very subtly and even then well mixed with the truth. A close look at some of the more prominent cults will show that a good portion, if not over half, of what they teach is true. A tare is one who has accepted error in place of truth and appears to be a believer outwardly but is in fact just an imitation of the genuine article. Men find it extremely difficult to cope with this type of "imitation", for it either contains much truth or it closely parallels the truth, making identification of error a nearly impossible task. It is on this ground that God says men are to keep their hands off and not to meddle in attempting to separate the two. It is not a task given to men to separate these one from another, for the parable goes on to say, "Let both grow together until the harvest -- at the end of the age." It will then be the responsibility of angels to assist in this separating task. God adds a little touch more to our understanding by saying " - - when the Lord Jesus shall be revealed from heaven with his mighty angels, In flaming fire taking vengeance on them that know not God, and obey not the gospel of our Lord Jesus Christ; - ." (II Thess. 1:7-8). This is a task the Holy Angels are far better equipped to perform than the best intentioned of men.

God says of these imitation believers "having a form of godliness, but denying the power of it; from such turn away." (II Tim. 3:5). Elsewhere He adds that the gospel is the power of God; when men refuse the truth of the gospel and instead substitute their own thoughts and desires it can only lead to self destruction.

*"For I am not ashamed of the gospel of Christ; for it is the power of God unto salvation to everyone that believeth; to the Jew first, and also to the Gentile." (Ro. 1:16).*

Tares are sown in the field which is said to be the world. (Matt. 13:38) Tares can and will appear in the local churches but they will never be found in the corporate Church, the mystical body of which Christ is the head. It requires a new birth by the Spirit of God for an individual to be placed as a member of the True Church. Being in the world, tares become a part of the Kingdom of Heaven which is shown to be a working world body politic. The Bible does not instruct believers to weed out the tares, not even the most obvious ones. Instead we are told just to turn away from them. The subject here is imitation Christians, whom some would call hypocrites; those who would like to appear to others as being very devout and religious. Tares are not referring to the pagans or to the unreligious who are the very ones to whom believers should be giving a strong witness in an attempt to win them to Christ.

There is a very close parallel between the teaching of this parable of the tares and that which is found to be true in the weekly worship services throughout all Christendom. There is not a man living who could go into a modern-day assembly of believers, and with any degree of accuracy, divide that congregation into groups of true believers and those who are just lip professors. If the rapture of the Church should occur today, many would be found occupying their regular seats in the pews of the local assemblies right through the weeks ahead. One of the great tragedies of the situation is that for some nearly whole denominations it would be business as usual without missing a beat. Despite the best intentions and the great effort expended by church boards and church memberships to screen applicants to prevent the acceptance of unbelievers, almost without exception, every local church membership roll has upon it the names of some individuals who have never been saved or truly born of the Spirit. Even those groups generally believed to be cults profess to be Christian and thus nominally speak of Christ as their King. There are true believers, those who possess Christ, and there are others who talk a good testimony but it is mere lip service only. This illustrates the truth that wheat and tares do exist side by side in the Kingdom of Heaven in its mystery form as it exists today. What is true of the kingdom of heaven in its mystery form is equally true of the kingdom in its actual form which is yet in the future. The book of Revelation teaches that after one thousand years of living under the righteous reign of Christ [known as the millennium] Satan is released from imprisonment and a multitude of men "as the sand of the sea" flock after him in the final rebellion against God. (Rev. 20:7-8). What greater proof than this that their heart wasn't right . They had a head knowledge but not a heart knowledge of God. They professed to know Christ but did not possess Him.

There is a vast difference between head knowledge and heart knowledge. Head knowledge amounts to intellectualism and can simply be the amassing together of a number of facts. Man's deepest emotions come from the heart. The writer of Proverbs recognized this as basic when he wrote "keep thy heart with diligence; for out of it are the issues of life." (Pro. 4:23). Men talk about "the affairs of the heart" when their thoughts turn to the subject of love, or marriage, or of family: all in a natural setting here on earth. There is but slight difference when talking on a spiritual level about love for God, or being a joint heir with Christ, or of the blessed hope that sustains us; for the emotions of the heart are involved in these matters also. The Bible says, "out of the abundance of the heart the mouth speaketh." (Matt. 12:34). The Apostle Paul laid it out quite plainly when he wrote,

> *"That if thou shalt confess with thy mouth Jesus as Lord, and shalt believe in thine heart that God hath raised him from the dead, thou shalt be saved. For with the heart man believeth unto righteousness; and with the mouth confession is made unto salvation." (Ro. 10:9-10).*

This last quotation brings into view the two root causes of most unbelief as well as the core of cultism. The first is the necessity to believe that Jesus is Lord (Deity). To believe He is any less than that is to believe in another Jesus; other than He whom the Bible reveals. (II Cor. 11:4). There are those who believe He was a great man, or that He was a great teacher, or even He was a great example -- for men to follow; but to believe He was God; no! they simply can't do that. Secondly the quotation says that one must believe Jesus was raised from the dead. The unbeliever says this is just demanding too much: everyone knows that death is final and no one has ever come back from the grave.

God is making a clear statement here that the mouth and the heart must be in harmony; the two must be as one if it is to be saving faith. One does not have to sit and listen long as his fellow man speaks before he can tell quite accurately how that individual regards spiritual things and the Word of God. If there is confession without evidence of faith it smacks of pure hypocrisy; if on the other side of the equation there is faith without confession -- it may be cowardice, or just plain pride. John wrote of an incident where this latter situation was an issue for he wrote,

> *"Nevertheless, among the chief rulers also many believed on him; but because of the Pharisees they did not confess him, lest they be put out of the synagogue; For they loved the praise of men more than the praise of God." (Jn. 12:42-43).*

When on earth the Lord sought to have men confess Him publicly; the Spirit seeks no less today.

# ILLUS. OF THE TARES
## THE KINGDOM OF HEAVEN

| Promised | At Hand | Rejected | (Mystery Form) | Established |
|---|---|---|---|---|
| II Sam 7:12-19 | Matt. 3:2 | Jn. 1:11 | Matt. 13: | Matt. 25:31-34 |

<u>Sower</u>  (————————)  <u>Tares</u> (————————) <u>Mustard Seed</u> (————————) (——

|  | <u>Wayside</u> | <u>Stony</u> | <u>Thorny</u> | <u>Good</u> |
|---|---|---|---|---|
| They All | hear | hear | hear | hear |
| Result | No understanding | No root | No fruit | Understanding |
| Enemy | Satan | Self | World | (Friend) H. S. |
| The Attack | Catch away | Offended | Choked | Bares Fruit |
|  |  |  |  |  |
| TheResult | <u>Unbelievers</u> | <u>Professors</u> | <u>Believers</u> | <u>Apostates</u> |
|  |  | Jn. 6:66 | Jn. 6:68-69 | Jn. 6:70-71 |

figure #3

*Chapter 2*

# THE PARABLE OF THE MUSTARD SEED SPEAKS OF UNNATURAL GROWTH.

*"Another parable put he forth unto them, saying, The kingdom of heaven is like a grain of mustard seed, which a man took, and sowed in his field; Which, indeed, is the least of all seeds; but when it is grown, it is the greatest among herbs, and becometh a tree, so that the birds of the air come and lodge in the branches of it." (Matt. 13:31-32)*

The third parable, that of the mustard seed, speaks of unnatural or even supernatural growth. Mustard is of a large family scientifically known as Brassicaceae, consisting of herbs and a few low shrubs. In this family there are about 215 genera and some 2000 species dispersed throughout the temperate zones of the earth being most abundant in Europe and Asia Minor. I can remember as a teenager working on my grandparents dairy farm in western Washington State that at certain times of the year the fields of hay would have great golden yellow patches in them from the maturing mustard. Mustard is normally a small plant or bush and the parable here speaks of it as abnormally growing into a great tree. An interesting phrase is used in the construction of this narrative when the mustard is said to grow from "the LEAST of all seeds --- to the GREATEST among herbs" and then continues on to become a tree. The comparison that Jesus is making can easily be seen when it is recalled that the kingdom of heaven had a very inauspicious beginning with one Leader and His twelve disciples. Today, two millennium later, "Christendom" is the largest or greatest religious entity on earth. According to the world almanac of 1989, Christendom claimed more than one billion adherents: the most among all the worlds major religions.

The parable goes on to say the mustard "tree" inadvertently becomes the shelter and the home of the birds of the air that come and light in its branches. To compound the issue this unnatural tree has a plethora of branches; just look at Christendom today in its much splintered, many-denominational glory. According to recent published statistics, there are actually hundreds of Protestant denominations in the

United States alone. In the Scriptures, birds are often used to denote that which is evil or bad. In the first parable as noted earlier in this study, it was birds that made away with the good seed which was interpreted as being the work of Satan or satanic in its purpose. Matt. 13:4,19. Another example of this is seen in the Book of Revelation where very strong language is used when it is stated that Babylon is fallen and had "become the habitation of demons, and the hold of every foul spirit, and a cage of every unclean and hateful bird." (Rev. 18:2). I personally have walked through vast acreages of corn fields and found almost every ear of corn damaged by birds. Farmers will testify that birds do an inestimable amount of damage to crops each year. One does not have to look very closely to see that "Christendom" today harbors many different birds. There are cults and "isms" everywhere the name of Christ is named. It also should be recognized that the birds are never a part of the tree but merely find shelter in it. The kingdom of heaven has this problem; it is plagued by the infestation of foul fowl.

## *THE PARABLE OF THE LEAVEN THE PERMEATING PRESENCE OF FALSE TEACHING.*

*"Another parable spoke he unto them, saying, The kingdom of heaven is like leaven, which a woman took, and hid in three measures of meal, till the whole was leavened." (Matt. 13:33).*

When looking at the parable of the leaven, an all pervasive influence can readily be detected. Leaven speaks of error, especially the error of false doctrine. Jesus warned on a number of occasions to "beware of the leaven of the pharisees" (Matt. 16:6) which His disciples soon came to understand to be the "doctrine" of the pharisees. Matt. 16:12. The same truth is reiterated in Luke's gospel in chapter twelve verse one when he gives a dire warning against the teaching of these religious leaders. The Apostle Paul, when writing to the church at Corinth, went a step further when he spoke of the leaven of "malice and wickedness," and he confirmed the truth of this fourth parable when he wrote "know ye not that a little leaven leaveneth the whole lump?" (I Cor. 5:6)

To restate the posit of this study, each of these parables reveals a truth that in the past ages was held in silence but is current today in the kingdom of heaven in its mystery form, as it also will be a factor of the millennial kingdom when it becomes a reality in the future. Christendom is a much divided or splintered fabrication with its many different branches, denominations, and yes, even sects. Mostly the divisions are brought about by differences of doctrine. This should be quite understandable when looking at the big picture. The field of Bible doctrine is very broad in its total range and has a number of distinctive sections that each alone would prove difficult to master. Just to name a few would be to list such as anthropology, hamartiology, soteriology, ecclesiology, eschatology, and Christology. There are a number of others that could be added to this short list, but the point is that any one of these would take years of study to even begin to master. Some students of the Word become proficient in a number of these areas but rare is the man who is proficient in all areas of Biblical doctrine or teaching. There always remain other areas that they are hardly able to touch if for no other reason than for lack of time to do so. We all know men of God who are experts in their field of study; men, we admire to. Let a man get out of his field of expertise and he can become just as big an embarrassment to the Christian community as a totally uneducated man. Would it be safe to say there are no two individuals that believe <u>all</u> the teachings of the Bible alike? If this be true, then somebody is in error. The Bible teaches that the leaven effects the <u>WHOLE</u> lump, there is no part that is left untouched. This would signify that no member or citizen of the kingdom of heaven is doctrinally pure or perfect. This fact can be seen quite readily in a number of different ways. It can be said no man has all the truth but will be constantly learning more as he reads and studies the Bible and the Holy Spirit gives him insight into the things he reads. It can equally be said that all a man believes of the Bible is not necessarily the truth. Each side of every controversy on bible doctrine, great or small, will have its adherents, and tragically, sometimes even unto death. It stands to reason that someone is in error — and certainly not impossible that all involved are. What is said here is equally true of those in the kingdom of God as well as true of every Church member. "A little leaven leveneth the whole lump."

## *The Parable of the HIDDEN TREASURE Israel: The Apple of His Eye.*

*"Again, the kingdom of heaven is like treasure hidden in a field, which when a man hath found, he hideth, and for joy of it goeth and selleth all that he hath, and buyeth that field." (Matt. 13:44)*

Continuing the study of the kingdom of heaven as it is revealed in Matthew chapter thirteen we now stop to peruse the parable of the hidden treasure. The treasure is said to be hidden in a field and earlier in this study we were explicitly told that "the field is the world." (Matt. 13:38) For the past three millennia, the one thing that has been hidden in the world is the Jewish race. They have not had a land of their own, until very recently in history, but have been scattered throughout all the nations, yet in spite of that obstacle have managed to retain their own identity. Jesus, when He came the first time, said He came "to seek and to save that which was lost." (Lk. 19:10) The Psalmist declared that the LORD had "chosen Israel for his peculiar treasure." (Psa. 135:4)

The parable goes on to reveal that the Seeker, after having found the treasure, rehid it, then went out and sold all that he possessed and bought, NOT the treasure, but the whole field in which the treasure was hidden. One of the best known verses in the Scriptures is referenced John 3:16 and it says "God so loved the world [the field] that he gave his only Son, ---" (the best that He had). Jesus died (not for His own sin) but for the sin of the whole world (I Jn. 1:7), so there is no excuse for any man not to receive and enjoy salvation.

Israel, that is the Jewish people, have rejected Jesus and they do not believe that He was or is their Messiah. Many of the Jews, if not most, still believe in their Messiah (Christ) and that he <u>WILL</u> come and deliver them from oppression. Believing that "The Christ" (not Jesus) is their coming king and deliverer fulfills the necessary criteria and thus includes Israel in the kingdom of heaven in its mystery form. Does it need to be said that at His second coming Jesus will be recognized and accepted as Israel's long looked for Messiah and at that time Israel will be the leading nation in the actual kingdom of heaven? All other nations will be blessed by and according to their relationship with that nation.

This is in no way implying that Israel is saved today. Israel is not a part of the church even though many individual Jews are. In this, the "church age," God is working with men one on one saving them as individuals, but nations are not being saved as nations. Each person, whether Jew or Gentile, must make a personal decision to accept Jesus as Savior and Lord, and when they do, they become citizens of the kingdom.

## *The Parable of the PEARL OF GREAT PRICE*
## *The Church: A Precious Jewel in His Sight.*

*"Again, the kingdom of heaven is like a merchant man, seeking fine pearls, Who, when he had found one pearl of great price, went and sold all that he had, and bought it".*
*(Matt. 13:45-46)*

This parable tells of a merchant man seeking pearls. Now a pearl is a jewel that is exceptional in its origin as well as in its makeup. It is not a mineral gem, but rather, it is the product of a living creature, the only jewel of this derivation; all other gems are made from minerals, and most therefore are crystalline in structure. A pearl is formed in stygian darkness in the depths of the sea. The Church also is the product of a living being; the Holy Spirit. It should at this point become very apparent to an astute student, the analogy between the forming of a pearl and the composition of the church, the body of Christ. It is an interesting study to see the illustrations that the Scriptures make of the sea.

*"The wicked are like the troubled sea, when it cannot rest, whose waters cast up mire and dirt, There is no peace, saith my God, to the wicked." (Isa. 57:20-21)*

> "The waters which thou sawest --- are peoples, and multitudes, and nations, and tongues." (Rev. 17:15)

Like the pearl formed at the bottom of the sea, these verses reveal with great accuracy the conditions and situations from which God is drawing out individuals from every nation under the sun to form His Church.

Furthermore, a pearl is formed because of suffering caused by an enemy object. A sharp grain of sand, the usual cause, gets inside the oyster's shell and there becomes the source of an irritation that is similar to an ulcer. The oyster in defense secretes layer upon layer of nacre around the object and thus the pearl is formed and grows bigger and bigger. Regardless of its size, a pearl is one single unit and to break this unity is to destroy the pearl. Every pearl has a foreign object at its core. In a parallel situation the church is being formed in like manner. The Bible says,

> "For when we were yet without strength, in due time Christ died for the ungodly." (Ro. 5:6)

> "But God commendeth his love toward us in that, while we were yet sinners, Christ died for us. Much more then, being justified by his blood, we shall be saved from wrath through him. For if, when we were enemies, we were reconciled to God by the death of his Son, much more, being reconciled, we shall be saved by his life." (Ro. 5:8-10).

The main thrust of the teaching of Matthew 13 concerns the Kingdom of Heaven, but with this parable of the pearl God brings to the fore front the body of the Church. It is well to remember that in the age in which we live God's top priority is the calling out of the Church, which is the "Bride of Christ." Only in a secondary manner is He interested in enlarging the Kingdom of God — though that is automatically taking place with each newly regenerated (born again) individual.

> "Jesus answered and said unto him, Verily, verily, I say unto thee, Except a man be born again, he cannot see the kingdom of God." (Jn. 3:3)

## Chapter 2

> *"For I would not, brethern, that ye should be ignorant of this mystery, — that blindness in part is happened to Israel until the fullness of the Gentiles be come in." (Ro. 11:25)*

> *"That the Gentiles should be fellow heirs, and of the same body, and partakers of his promise in Christ by the gospel." (Eph. 3:6)*

There are vast numbers of men and women who call themselves "Christian" who are neither members of the True Church nor citizens of the Kingdom of God but they do meet the criteria to be called citizens of the Kingdom of Heaven. It may come as a surprise to many but the living generation of the True Church has a real and viable part to play in the Kingdom of Heaven in this the mystery age. The gist of what is being taught here is that every "born again" person has a distinct place in three different parts of God's great plan of the ages. First and foremost, he is a member of the True Church, the Bride of Christ, and the Holy Spirit indwells him. Secondly, he becomes a citizen of the spiritual Kingdom of God and joins with all the servants of God of past ages. Thirdly, he becomes a citizen of the Kingdom of Heaven on earth with instructions to live holy, produce good works, and be a witness to the Living God here and now.

> *"Who hath delivered us from the power of darkness, and hath translated us into the kingdom of his dear Son;" (Col. 1:13).*

For generation after generation God has been adding new believers to His church and will continue to do so until the church is complete, At that time, just as the pearl is brought up from darkness at the bottom of the sea into the light, so the church will be caught up, raptured, into the glorious presence of the Lord. A pearl requires the touch of life to stay brilliant, and it will grow "sick" and lusterless if not worn. After the Church is "caught up" and taken from the earth, she will receive her glorious apparel and then the marriage with the Lamb will occur in heaven. Standing by the side of the Bridegroom, the Church will be seen by the whole creation in all her glory and beauty. Following this God will once again turn His attention to the bringing to fruition the Kingdom of Heaven on earth and there the Church will be seen sitting at the side of Christ, ruling and reigning with Him.

## The Parable of the DRAG NET
## The Net Does Not Discriminate in What It Catches.

> *"Again, the kingdom of heaven is like a net, that was cast into the sea, and gathered of every kind, Which, when it was full, they drew to shore, and sat down, and gathered the good into vessels, but cast the bad away. So shall it be at the end of the age; the angels shall come forth, and separate the wicked from among the righteous, And shall cast them into the furnace of fire; --" (Matt. 13:47-50).*

This final parable of Matthew thirteen, that of the drag net, is a familiar simile to all those that live near the coast. It is a common sight, a favorite pastime, to watch commercial fishermen set out a purse seine net, then close it and haul in the catch of fish. One of the first things to be brought to our attention is that the net is cast into the sea which, in the study of the parable preceding this one, was seen to represent masses of people or the nations of the world. When the net was full, not before, it was brought to shore and found to have caught fish of various kinds, both good and bad. The message here is familiar because it is a repetition of that given in the second parable. The citizenry that comprise the Kingdom of Heaven includes both wheat and tares, good fish and bad, and the separation of the two does not take place until the end of the age. Even then, it is not the responsibility of men to do the separating but it is shown to be a heavenly undertaking with the angels doing the work at the Lord's instruction. God's Word says,

> *"For the LORD seeth not as man seeth; for man looketh on the outward appearance, but the LORD looketh on the heart."* (I Sam. 16:7).

The truth being revealed here is of such importance that God thought it necessary to repeat it for greater emphasis. Men simply are incapable of distinguishing the saved from the unsaved. Inestimable damage has been done by men who step in and for whatever reason try to do that which God's Word says they are not equipped to do. The parable of the tares said "let both grow together until the harvest" and the parable of the net says that the separating will be done at "the end of the age." Both of these parables emphasize that the angels will be the ones to do the separating. It is a good thing to keep in mind that the subject being dealt with here is the Kingdom of Heaven and not the Church. The Bible never indicates at any time that there are ever tares or bad fish in the true Church, the spotless Bride of Christ. At this point it should be brought to mind that tares are an imitation or a mere look-a-like of the real thing.

It may be concluded through the compilation of truth contained in these seven parables that everyone, in this the mystery age, who professes to own Christ as their unseen King is in the Kingdom of Heaven in its mystery form.

*figure #4*

*Chapter III*

# THE MYSTERIES OF THE KINGDOM OF GOD

## The Spiritual Kingdom that Incorporates All Godly Creatures of All Time.

*"And he said unto them, Unto you it is given to know the mystery of the kingdom of God; but unto those who are outside, all these things are done in parables, --"  (Mk. 4:11).*

A very effective method of study is that done by way of comparison; to bring two different things into view at the same time that the similarities and the diversities may be readily seen. It is my intention to do so now in this study and bring into focus a second kingdom, that of the Kingdom of God, and show that it is separate and diverse from the Kingdom of Heaven of which we have been studying. First and foremost the Scriptures say that in our age or generation unless a man is "born again" he will never see or never enter the Kingdom of God.

*"Jesus answered and said unto him, verily, verily, I say unto thee, except a man be born again, he cannot see the kingdom of God." (Jn. 3:3).*

*"Jesus answered, verily, verily, I say unto thee, except a man be born of water and of the Spirit, he cannot enter into the kingdom of God. That which is born of the flesh is flesh; and that which is born of the Spirit is Spirit. Marvel not that I said unto thee, ye MUST be born again." (Jn. 3:5-7).*

These quotations lead to the conclusion that the Kingdom of God is spiritual and is on an altogether different basis or level than the Kingdom of Heaven. The Kingdom of God is not confined to just the living, nor to the earth, nor to men. The Bible informs us that the Old Testament saints who have passed on from this earthly scene are in the Kingdom of God.

> *"There shall be weeping and gnashing of teeth, when you shall see Abraham, Isaac, and Jacob, and all the prophets in the kingdom of God, and you yourselves thrust out." (Lk. 13:28).*

Scripture everywhere reveals that God is sovereign and His authority extends throughout the entire universe covering all intelligences, angels and men. The Kingdom of God is found wherever loyal subjection to that authority is found. For men it is a case of either enter the Kingdom of God or face hell fire.

> *"If thine eye offend thee, pluck it out; it is better for thee to enter into the kingdom of God with one eye than, having two eyes, to be cast into hell fire." (Mk. 9:47).*

Of the seven parables given in relation to the Kingdom of Heaven in Matthew chapter thirteen only three of them are repeated elsewhere as having a like relation to the Kingdom of God. These three are 1) the parable of the sower; (Mk. 4:1-25) 2) the parable of the mustard seed; (Mk. 4:30-32) 3) and the parable of the leaven. (Lk. 13:20-21). Many readers come to the conclusion that because these three parables are applied to both the Kingdom of Heaven and the Kingdom of God that it is implied the two names are optional and there is only one kingdom being spoken of in the Gospels. Such a conclusion may be in grave error. The four parables that are used to describe aspects of the Kingdom of Heaven and <u>not</u> those of the Kingdom of God can be of far greater significance than the former three. To the astute mind the differences seem more important than the similarities.

The Scriptures show that a new birth, that is a Spiritual birth, is essential to entrance by men into the realm where God's authority is unquestioned; namely the Kingdom of God. This alone rules out the presence of either "tares" or "scrap fish." Nor could Israel, The Hidden

Treasure, be included in the Kingdom of God for they have rejected and continue to reject Jesus as their Messiah King. In the age in which we are living, nations are <u>not</u> being saved: individuals are. God is working with men on a one on one basis. This thought that God is working with individuals, one at a time, with the end result being a new (spiritual) birth would seem to be placing the most emphasis on God's work of building the Church. According to the New Testament, regeneration, a new birth, establishes the recipient in both areas of God's present ongoing work; the Kingdom of God, (Jn. 3:3) and in the Church. Today, in this present age, God's top priority is upon the Church; not on the kingdom. He is calling out a "bride" for His Son. While believers are made citizens of the Kingdom of God, this relationship remains secondary to the more important and higher calling of God as each believer becomes a member of the corporate body of Christ; the Church. It is because of this connection that each believer may lay claim to the precious promises that God has reiterated through the Apostle Paul when he wrote,

> *"Blessed be the God and Father of our LORD Jesus Christ, who hath blessed us with <u>all</u> spiritual blessings in heavenly places in Christ: According as he hath chosen us in him before the foundation of the world, that we should be holy and <u>without</u> blame before him, — "  (Eph. 1:3-4)*

> *"To the praise of the glory of his grace, through which he hath made us <u>accepted</u> in the Beloved; In whom we have redemption through his blood, the forgiveness of sins, according to the riches of his grace, — "  (Eph. 1:6-7).*

For one to say Israel is not in the Kingdom of God is often apt to raise the cry of anti-Semitism but nevertheless is a basic truth this portion of God's Word makes quite clear. The church on earth also, as far as the local assemblies are concerned, harbor in their memberships, tares, those who have never experienced a new birth and thus the parable of the Pearl of Great Price is likewise omitted from a description of the Kingdom of God. The reality of the situation is the sad fact that to the world of the unsaved the local church is the only means they have to form an opinion of the power and veracity of the Living God.

It is a fact that entrance into either of the two kingdoms comes <u>ONLY</u> by hearing the Word of God; but the Scriptures <u>NEVER</u> relate that there are tares in the Kingdom of God as there are in the Kingdom of Heaven. The difference between the two is that for entrance into the Kingdom of God not only is it required that the individual hear the Word but he must act upon what he hears and become obedient to it. The key to understanding the difference of the requirements to these two kingdoms is the principle of commitment or obedience. For a man to enter the Kingdom of God he must act upon what he hears and believes. The grasp of intellectual knowledge alone is not sufficient; it must become experiential knowledge. Only then will the entrance to the Kingdom of God, the domain where God reigns as sovereign, be thrown wide open and the believer unreservedly be received and accepted. It has been mentioned that the main theme running through the gospel of Matthew is "the King and His Kingdom" and this referring to the earthly Kingdom of Heaven. Matthew does not vary from this theme in all twenty eight chapters, yet for all that, in the middle of his lengthy discourse, he pauses in chapter six to say,

*"But seek ye <u>FIRST</u> the kingdom of God, and his righteousness, and all these things will be added unto you." (Matt. 6:33).*

This should irrefutably establish superior position and higher priority for the Kingdom of God over that of the Kingdom of Heaven. After all Jesus did say "ye <u>MUST</u> be born again."

An area seldom discussed and even less seldom preached or taught upon is that transition period that exists between physical death and the future resurrection. A believer, once he leaves this life, is no longer a member of the Kingdom of Heaven in its mystery form, for that kingdom is on earth. It is true, he is a member of the Church but that body is not yet complete and thus is not ready to be put on exhibition before all the universe as it will be one day. The Scripture says "to be absent from the body, and (is) to be present with the Lord." (II Cor. 5:8). This is the period when membership in the Kingdom of God comes into prominence. The believer is at once in unity and fellowship with the Old Testament saints and even with the Holy Angels. We will be in the presence of Almighty God and we will experience much the same scene

*Chapter 3*

that the prophet Isaiah saw and recorded in the sixth chapter of his prophecy.

When the Church is complete and is physically raptured into the presence of the Lord, the marriage of the Lamb takes place. (Rev. 19:7). After this the Lord, with the Church, returns to the earth to install the Millenial Kingdom. (Rev. 19:11-16). It is during this time the Church will be found ruling and reigning with Christ for the one-thousand year period. (Rev. 20:6). Following the Millenial Kingdom all authority will be turned over to God the Father and the Kingdom of God will be in full flower for all future eternity. (I Cor. 15:28).

## Chapter IV
## *THE MYSTERY OF THE WISDOM OF GOD*

*"We speak the wisdom of God in a mystery, even the hidden wisdom, which God ordained before the ages unto our glory."*
*(I Cor. 2:7).*

As we approach the subject of the wisdom of God I would like by way of introduction to bring attention to several passages written by that man of wisdom, King Solomon, as recorded in the book of Proverbs.

*"My son, if thou wilt receive my words and lay up my commandments with thee, So that thou incline thine ear unto wisdom, and apply thine heart to understanding; Yea, if thou criest after knowledge, and liftest up thy voice for understanding; If thou seekest her as silver, and searchest for her as for hidden treasures; Then shalt thou understand the fear of the LORD, and find the knowledge of God. For the LORD giveth wisdom; out of his mouth cometh knowledge and understanding."*
*(Pro. 2:1-6).*

*"Get wisdom, get understanding; forget it not, neither decline from the words of my mouth. Forsake her not, and she shall preserve thee; love her, and she shall keep thee. Wisdom is the principal thing; therefore, get wisdom; and with all thy getting, get understanding." (Pro. 4:5-7).*

*"The fear of the LORD is the beginning of wisdom, and the knowledge of the Holy One is understanding." (Pro. 9:10).*

From these Scriptures it is easy to see that understanding and wisdom are to be considered priceless; that both come to us from God and should be sought after at any or all cost. It is sometimes very easy for men to attain knowledge, vast knowledge, but the wisdom to use that knowledge is quite another thing.

The schools and universities in America can impart a vast amount of knowledge in an incredible variety of subjects but in doing so they fail in any attempt to include even a particle of wisdom in the learning process. This commodity, wisdom, is attained through experience when a person either consciously or unconsciously incorporates Judeo-Christian principles (ethics) into his daily living experiences. Most civil governments have found this fact to be true and they have shaped their basic laws around these same principles whether they were aware of their origin or not. Wisdom is entirely separate from knowledge and is defined as "an understanding of that which is right, true, and lasting." In the past several score of years knowledge has increased greatly; having more than doubled. A full set of encyclopedias can become obsolete in a very short period of time. The story is completely different; almost a reversal is seen when approaching the subject of wisdom. The world of men, much to their chagrin, has indeed found wisdom to be in extremely short supply.

Man places a very high priority on education and supposedly only the most brilliant and best educated people are chosen or appointed to lofty positions of authority in business or government. Despite this positioning of the highly educated, those people who have obtained great knowledge, the record clearly shows there have been catastrophic failures in nearly every aspect of modern society; in the area of primary education, in banking, in commerce, in law, in business, etc. There has been an unbelievable series of convoluted judgments and decisions that defy all rational reasoning, that have been and are being foisted off on the public. These without a doubt are cases of knowledge without wisdom. Not long ago there appeared an article in public print that gave ample reason for a person to stop and meditate on the situation. In the course of the written statement the author wrote, "there is no apparent lack of educated —— fools." This can be seen as a very blunt and harsh assessment of current affairs but nevertheless it strikes close to being on target as a direct hit.

The Bible says "The fool saith in his heart, there is no God." (Psa. 14:1) For one to leave God out of his life altogether; out of family, business, work, pleasure, all else, is to be cut loose from all absolutes. Everything becomes relative. It is God who set standards whether they be moral, ethical, truth, good, evil, or any other. True wisdom begins with God. The wise man who wrote the Book of Proverbs said, "The way of a fool is right in his own eyes, but he that hearkeneth unto counsel is wise." (Pro. 12:15) As quoted before in this essay the godly man who wrote the Proverbs said, "The fear of the LORD is the beginning of wisdom, — " (Pro. 9:10) The word fear as used here does not mean dread or trepidation but rather awe, reverential awe, a recognition of God as being Sovereign. Truth is always truth whether it is accepted or not. Those who know the Lord in a personal and intimate manner know the validity of Jesus' promise when He said "And you shall know the truth, and the truth shall make you free." (Jn. 8:32) A wise man of the past wrote,

> *"Let the wicked forsake his way, and the unrighteous man his thoughts, and let him return unto the LORD, and he will have mercy upon him; and to our God; for he will abundantly pardon. For my thoughts are not your thoughts, neither are your ways my ways, saith the LORD. For as the heavens are higher than the earth, so are my ways higher than your ways, and my thoughts than your thoughts." (Isa. 55:7-9)*

From the beginning of time there have been numerous problems that have continued to plague mankind. Among these problems none have been greater or more persistent than three that were put into words by probably the first of the writers that God used to produce the Scriptures. The author that I refer to is Job, who undoubtedly was not the first man to wrestle with the problems of life. These three questions have certainly been asked by men of every generation since his time. Yet because Job stated the problems so precisely, I will quote his words.

*Problem #1 "How should man be just before God?" (Job 9:2, 25:4).*

*Problem #2 "If a man die, shall he live again?" (Job 14:14).*

*Problem #3 "Oh, that I knew where I might find him, that I might come even to his seat." (Job 23:3).*

These represent the most serious questions and the deepest desires with which the minds of men can grapple. We are living in the time or age in which it has pleased God to reveal the answers to these basic questions. The answers come through the understanding of what was accomplished in the work and ministry of the incarnate Son of God, Jesus Christ. God knows all about the problems with which man has so ineffectively wrestled down through the years. In His master plan He predetermined that His own Son, Jesus, would enter man's domain and in doing so, would provide the solution for the problems with which sinful man was so unable to cope. The Bible says, "When the fullness of the time was come, God sent forth his Son, made of a woman, made under the law, to redeem them who were under the law ---" (Gal. 4:4).

Jesus came right on schedule, exactly as God had planned, not a day too soon nor a day too late. He came that the race of men might have the true and proper answers to the questions that so disturbed and baffled them. Looking at the context of I Corinthians chapter two of which the text (verse seven) is taken for this section of our study, we read,

*"Eye hath not seen, nor ear heard, neither have entered into the heart of man, the things which God has prepared for them that love him. But God has revealed them unto us by his Spirit; for the Spirit searches all things, yea, the deep things of God. --- Now we have received, not the spirit of the world, but the Spirit who is of God; that we might <u>KNOW</u> the things that are freely given to us of God." (I Cor. 2:9-12).*

God planned that Jesus Christ would supply the answers to all of men's unsolved problems. Verse nine speaks of "things that God has prepared for them that love him", things that lift sinners from sin, corruption, and death to everlasting glory. Jesus said, "Henceforth I call you not servants; for the servant knoweth not what his lord doeth; but I have called you friends; for <u>all things</u> that I have heard of my Father I have <u>made known</u> unto you." (Jn. 15:15).

## *Answer to Problem #1*

How did Jesus supply the answers to the problems that Job verbalized? First, Jesus came to give Himself as a sacrifice for us, to die in our place as our substitute, for our sin. "Herein is love, not that we loved God, but that he loved us, and sent his Son to be the propitiation for our sins." (I Jn. 4:10). "And he is the propitiation for our sins, and not for ours only, but also for the sins of the whole world." (I Jn. 2:2).

PROPITIATION: the key thought in this word is that of "satisfaction" --- God being satisfied with the payment made for the disposal of sin. Jesus' sacrifice of Himself answered all the just demands of God's holiness against sin, and God declared Himself satisfied. The problem of sin before God has been settled forever. God will never again demand further payment for sin from the sinner, <u>ANY</u> sinner. If men perish it will not be because of their sin but it will be caused by their unbelief. The Bible says, "-- that God was in Christ reconciling the <u>WORLD</u> unto himself, not <u>IMPUTING</u> (charging) their trespasses unto them, and hath committed unto us the word of reconciliation." (II Cor. 5:19). God is not charging men's sins against them; He has already charged these sins to Jesus Christ and Jesus paid the full price --- every thing that God demanded. The sufficiency of the price paid for the ransom of men can be seen for the following reasons: 1) it was a blood sacrifice involving a human life; 2) the offerer was sinless, being free from contamination through Adam's seed, this as a result of the Virgin birth; and 3) being the Son of God, He was infinite. The value of His infinite life was greater than the sum total of all finite human lives.

## *Answer to Problem #2*

Is their life after death? The answer to this question is also found in the life and work of Jesus Christ. The Bible says, "Just as sin entered the world through one man, and death by sin, and in this way death came to all men, because all sinned." (Ro. 5:12) NIV. To this ominous portent the Bible adds as a result of Jesus' work,

> *"Just as the result of one trespass was condemnation for all men, so also the result of one act of righteousness was justification that brings life for all men. For just as through the disobedience of the one man the many were made sinners, so also through the obedience of the one man the many will be made righteous." (Ro. 5:18-19) NIV.*

This is the time to bring into view one of the deeper, more profound truths God has so graciously given to us; this one from the pen of the Apostle Paul while he was writing concerning Jesus being raised from the dead. "Who was delivered for our offences, and was raised again for our justification." (Ro. 4:25). Most bible teachers and bible commentators have no problem with the first phrase of this often quoted verse. If we substitute, and rightly so, the word "because" in place of the existing "for" there is a clear understanding of the generally accepted meaning of the phrase. He was delivered, or He died, because of our offenses. This is very true and a vital point of the gospel. The second phrase of this short verse is an entirely different story. Here many commentaries interpret this to mean that because He was raised from the dead we are, or can be, justified. If as in the case of the first phrase, we again substitute because in place of this second for, we have this reading, "He was raised again because of our justification," This makes good solid sense.

Let's follow through on this line of truth. God said "the wages of sin is death." (Ro. 3:23). He further states that His Son, Jesus, died in our place for our sin. (Ro. 5:8). The <u>death</u> of Christ completely satisfied God's holiness in its demands against sin. The Bible does not say the wages of sin is suffering, or sorrow, or remorse. Sin is not washed away in a flood of tears. Sin can only be removed by legal or judicial fiat and God said "the wages of sin is death". The Bible then reveals that a substitute, Christ, died in our place. Our debt was paid —totally — in full. Our sin is GONE — removed as far as the east is from the west. (Psa. 103:12). God has no further demands against us — none. We are justified. What happens to a debt that is paid? Does one wrap it up and store it away on a shelf or in a drawer for some future use? If it is a very large debt, is it crated up and trucked to some convenient place for storage? NO! When a debt is paid it is gone, cancelled, wiped out. That is exactly what happened to our sin when Jesus paid the complete price that God's holiness demanded.

With His death the load of our sin and guilt that had been dumped on Him has been removed, all of it, and since it is no longer there to keep Jesus Christ in the grave - - - <u>HE AROSE</u>. Because He arose, we who are in Christ shall arise also. There is no longer a heavy load of sin on the individual believer; that was transferred to Christ and was subsequently paid for and removed. It is gone, never to confront us again. We are free. Now He is the forerunner who has gone on ahead and opened the way to the Father for us. Where He has gone we can and will follow. (Heb. 6:20) "There is, therefore, now no condemnation to them who are in Christ Jesus, — (Ro. 8:1) "Verily, verily, I say unto you, he that heareth my word, and believeth on him that sent me, hath everlasting life, and shall not come into judgment, but is passed from death unto life." (Jn. 5:24).

## *Answer to Problem #3*

How do sinfull men approach a holy God seated on His throne in glory? Like the others, this problem too has its solution in the work of Jesus the Christ in that which was accomplished in His first visit to earth. He said,

*"I am the way, the truth, and the life; no man cometh unto the Father, (God) but by me." (Jn. 14:6).*

The Bible teaches, especially in the book of Hebrews, that the work of a priest is to make access to God for men. This is precisely the goal that Jesus purposed to accomplish when He came to earth as a man born of the virgin Mary. He took all of man's sin as well as all of his sins upon Himself and thus through His voluntary, substitutionary death He paid all that was required by God's holiness as the price for freedom from these things. As a direct result of Jesus' death, and through an act of faith on the part of the individual, men are justified; that is, they are declared to be righteous, thus they are fit to enter the presence of the holy, living God.

The wisdom of God is expressly exhibited in His ability to solve the human race's most knotty issues. Those complex problems that have baffled men for centuries find ready solutions in the things God has worked out and finished if men would only listen and accept, or believe. The New Testament words it this way,

> *"In order that the manifold wisdom of God might now be made known through the church to the rulers and the authorities in the heavenly places. This was in accordance with the eternal purpose which He carried out in Christ Jesus our LORD, in whom we have boldness and confident access through faith in Him." (Eph. 3:10-12). NASB*

When it comes to the question of every day decisions the best resource the individual may have is an acquaintance or relationship with the LORD Jesus Christ. Once a man becomes a believer and accepts the salvation God so freely offers, the Spirit of Christ becomes resident in that believer's life. With this residency comes all the benefits of the wisdom of God and they are freely placed at the believer's disposal. This blessing alone is of great advantage to every true Christian.

> *"but we preach Christ crucified, — unto them who are called, — Christ the power of God, <u>and the wisdom of God</u>. Because the foolishness of God is wiser than men; and the weakness of God is stronger than men." (I Cor. 1:23-25).*

*Chapter V*

# THE MYSTERY OF THE GOSPEL

*This mystery reveals the power of God in the gospel in making sinners into saints and placing them as members into the body of Christ; The Church.*

*"Praying always with all prayer and supplication in the Spirit, and watching there unto with all perseverance and supplication for all saints; and for me, that utterance may be given unto me, that I may open my mouth boldly to make known the <u>mystery of the gospel,</u> for which I am an ambassador in bonds; that I may speak boldly, as I ought to speak." (Eph. 6:18-20).*

To speak of the gospel as being a New Testament mystery may come as a surprise to many. There are a number of different gospels spoken of in the Bible: 1) The Gospel of the Kingdom, which was preached by the Lord during His ministry here on earth. (Matt. 4:23). 2) The Gospel of Jesus Christ, (Mk. 1:1); 3) The Everlasting Gospel, which will be preached by an angel. (Rev. 14:6); and 4) The one the Apostle Paul referred to as "MY GOSPEL." (Ro. 2:16, 16:25). The word gospel comes from the old English "god-spell" which meant good tidings and is the English equivalent of the Greek word "evaggelion." The first four books of the New Testament are known as the four Gospels and attached to each is the name of its author: the Gospel of Matthew, the Gospel of Mark, etc. There was a period of about four hundred years of silence between the last of the Old Testament prophets and the coming of Jesus, The Messiah, as reported in these four gospels. The angelic announcement of His coming was the cause of great excitement in some quarters in Israel. The four Gospels give the account of His birth, His teaching, His work including miracles, His suffering, His substitutionary death, His resurrection, His ascension, and His promise to return. This is glad tidings of the very highest caliber. Much of what the four Gospels relate is the fulfillment of prophecy that was given in the Old Testament, many centuries in the past. Glad tidings indeed! -- but certainly not in the category of a New Testament mystery. The message given is proof positive that God had not given up on His creature, man, by simply abandoning him to his fate. Of equal significance is the message's announcement that the Messiah would be named "Emmanuel," God with us. Matt. 1:23. These four authors give to the world the only true and authentic knowledge of Jesus that is to be had.

The writer of the first Gospel, Matthew, whose theme is "Jesus: the King and His kingdom", is the author who gives to the world the most information on "the gospel of the kingdom." (Matt. 4:23) This is the gospel that both John the Baptist and Jesus preached. Because Jesus was a man, He was limited by the body of a man, and thus He had a very restricted ministry. He and the twelve disciples He trained, ministered only to Israel, for Matthew writes,

> *"These twelve Jesus sent forth, and commanded them, saying, Go not into the way of the Gentiles, and into any city of the Samaritans enter not; But go, rather, to the lost sheep of the house of Israel. And as ye go, preach, saying, The kingdom of heaven is at hand." (Matt. 10:5-7).*

Immediately following the Lord's personal ministry here on earth, two events took place which had tremendous impact on the human race. The first was the advent of the Holy Spirit, when He came to the earth and began His resident ministry. Prior to this event, the Spirit came and went as His ministry required as He worked with men. He often came upon men to empower them for specific work, but it was never said that He indwelt them. One of the stipulations Jesus made concerning His departure was that the Spirit would come, and that He would become a permanent fixture in the life of every believer.

> *"And I will pray the Father, and he shall give you another Comforter, that he may abide with you forever;" ( Jn. 14:16).*

## Chapter 5

> *"But the Comforter, who is the Holy Spirit, whom the Father will send in my name, —"* (Jn. 14:26). *"Nevertheless, I tell you the truth: It is expedient for you that I go away; for if I go not away, the Comforter will not come unto you; but if I depart, I will send him unto you."* (Jn. 16:7).

The Holy Spirit, without the limitations of a human body, was sent to minister to the entire human race, not just to Israel. One of the attributes of the Spirit of God is omnipresence: He is everywhere present all the time. This fact alone would dictate that His ministry would be expanded to include all men, worldwide, not just one small nation. The Psalmist understood the potential work of the Spirit for he said, "Whither shall I go from thy Spirit? Or whither shall I flee from thy presence? If I ascend up into heaven, thou art there; if I make my bed in sheol, behold, thou art there." (Psa. 139:7-8).

The second great event to be considered is that, with the new and enlarged ministry came a new message, a new gospel. Closely accompanying the close of Jesus' ministry on earth, a contemporary of His whom the world has come to know as the Apostle Paul, was chosen by God for a unique life of service. This man had come to a face to face experience with the Lord and his life was completely -- changed. This world will probably never again see a man so wholly dedicated to the work the Lord called him to do. God was able by revelation to give Paul an entirely new gospel. Paul wrote,

> *"For this reason I, Paul, -- if indeed you have heard of the stewardship of God's grace which was given to me for you; that by revelation there was made known to me the mystery, as I wrote before in brief. And by referring to this, when you read you can understand my insight into the mystery of Christ, which in other generations was not made known to the sons of men, as it has now been revealed -- "* (Eph. 3:1-5). NASB

Paul not only received this message but he had the ability to systematically record what he heard and learned. Just as in the distant past, God gave a distinct message at Mt. Sinai and it came to be known by a man's name, the law of Moses, even so, this new message also carries the name of the man God used to disseminate it: Paul's gospel.

When referring to the new revelation that God had given him, Paul called it "my Gospel." (Ro. 2:16). It is this last mentioned gospel -- Paul's Gospel -- to which I wish to draw attention. While writing to the Saints in the church at Ephesus he refers to it as "the gospel of your salvation", (Eph. 1:13) and that is the name I will adhere to throughout the remainder of the study.

The gospel of salvation as it is preached and taught during this church age, contains five cardinal points. If any one of these five points is excluded or eliminated this gospel is made of no effect. There may be many other points -- points of secondary importance -- that may or may not be emphasized, but these five make the gospel. The five are:

1) *"that Christ died for our sins according to the scriptures."* *(I Cor. 15:3).*

2) *"and that he was buried,"* *(I Cor. 15:4).*

3) *"and that he rose again the third day according to the scriptures."* *(I Cor. 15:4).*

4) *"Ye must be born again"* -- Regeneration *(John 3:7).*

5) The Indwelling of the Holy Spirit *(John 14:16-18).*

The gospel of salvation is for the church and is preached in the church age only. Jesus, in His ministry here on the earth did not preach this gospel of salvation but rather, He preached the gospel of the kingdom as is clearly stated in Matthew 4:23, 9:35. Not one of the five major points of the gospel of salvation can be found in Jesus' sermon preached on the "Mount" in Matthew chapter five, nor in the "Beatitudes" given in the same chapter.

The church had its beginning during the events that took place during Pentecost -- fifty days after the death and resurrection of Jesus. The promised Comforter of John 16:7, the Holy Spirit, did not come, indeed could not have come, until after the Lord Jesus ascended back to His Father. (Acts 1:4, 8) It was only with the advent of the Holy Spirit that men began to experience regeneration, as He began His ministry of indwelling believers and bringing them into the body of Christ, the

Church. Even Jesus' disciples, those who walked and talked with Him, who learned from His teaching in His three year ministry, were not regenerated until the tremendous events that took place on Pentecost.

> *"And when the day of Pentecost was fully come, they were all with one accord in one place. And suddenly there came a sound from heaven like a rushing mighty wind, and it filled all the house where they were sitting. And there appeared unto them cloven tongues as of fire, and it sat upon each of them. And they were all filled with the Holy Spirit, ---"* (Acts 2:1-4).

From the very beginning of the church age, effective sermons contained the cardinal points of the gospel of salvation. The Apostle Paul may be the man the Lord chose to codify or systematize this gospel of salvation but the Apostle Peter used it with great success. Even a most cursory inspection of the first sermons recorded in the Book of Acts reveal this to be true. Peter's words in Acts chapter two contained these major truths of this gospel.

> *"Ye men of Israel, hear these words: Jesus of Nazareth, a man approved of God among you by miracles and wonders and signs, which God did by him in the midst of you, as ye yourselves know; Him, being delivered by the determinate counsel and foreknowledge of God, ye have taken, and by wicked hands have <u>crucified and slain</u>; Whom God hath <u>raised up</u>, having loosed the pains of death, because it was not possible that he should be held by it."* (Acts 2:22-24)

> *"This Jesus hath God <u>raised up</u>, whereof we all are witnesses. Therefore, being by the right hand of God exalted, and having received from the Father the promise of the Holy Spirit, he hath shed forth this, which ye now see and hear."* (Acts 2:32-33)

> *"Then Peter said unto them, Repent, and be baptized, every one of you, in the name of Jesus Christ for the remission of sins, and <u>ye shall receive the gift of the Holy Spirit</u>. For the promise is unto you, and to your children, and to all that are afar off, even as many as the Lord, our God, shall call."* (Acts 2:38-39).

Furthermore, when Peter spoke to the multitude at the gate of the temple following the healing of the lame man, these same truths were again made evident.

> *"'But ye denied the Holy One and the Just, and desired a murderer to be granted unto you; And <u>killed the Prince of Life</u>, whom God hath <u>raised from the dead</u>, of which we are witnesses.'" (Acts 3:14-15)*
>
> *"Then Peter, filled with the Holy Spirit, said unto them, — 'Be it known unto you all, and to all the people of Israel, that by the name of Jesus Christ of Nazareth, <u>whom ye crucified</u>, whom <u>God raised from the dead</u>, even by him doth this man stand here before you' — And when they had prayed, the place was shaken where they were assembled together; and they were all <u>filled with the Holy Spirit</u>, — " (Acts 4:8, 10, 31).*

The resurrection from among the dead has become a unique doctrine of the church, and it is this doctrine in particular that makes Christianity different from any and all other faiths among men. Peter did not abandon the formula for successful soul winning when he first was sent to the gentiles and spoke in the house of Cornelius. What proved good for the Jews proved to be just as good and effective for the gentiles, for the Bible says:

> *"Then Peter opened his mouth, and said, 'Of a truth I perceive that God is no respecter of persons; -- And we are witnesses of all things which he did, both in the land of the Jews and in Jerusalem: whom <u>they slew</u> and hanged on a tree. Him <u>God raised up the third day</u>, and showed him openly:' While Peter yet spoke these words, <u>the Holy Spirit fell on all them</u> who heard the word." (Acts 10:34, 39-40, 44).*

The Apostle Paul was obedient to the same impetus that compelled Peter, for he too recognized the importance and the power in the message of a resurrected Lord and did not hesitate to declare it. Paul's message, centered around the truth that the Spirit of the One who was victorious over death, is the same One that is given to indwell every believer. His letter to the church in Rome stated his message and his purpose very concisely right from the opening words.

> *"Paul, a servant of Jesus Christ, called to be an apostle, separated unto the <u>gospel of God</u> -- Concerning his Son, Jesus Christ our Lord, -- And declared to be the Son of God with power, according to the spirit of holiness, by the <u>resurrection from the dead</u>; By whom we have received grace and apostleship, for obedience to the faith among all nations, for his name;"*
> (Ro. 1:1-5)

Early in his ministry while on his first missionary journey in what is now the nation of Turkey, Paul was speaking in a Jewish synagogue and preaching Jesus. He said:

> *"-- They that dwell at Jerusalem, and their rulers, - - though they found no cause of death in him, yet desired they Pilate that <u>he should be slain</u>. And when they had fulfilled all that was written of him, they took him down from the tree, and <u>laid him in a sepulcher</u>. But <u>God raised him from the dead</u>."*
> (Acts 13:27-30)

Later in his journeys while traveling in Europe, Paul was confronted by Greek philosophers during a stop at Athens. These men of Athens were known for their cynicism and scorn for all others. Even here Paul did not change his tactics or his message, but strongly and clearly proclaimed the gospel of salvation.

> *"-- Paul - disputed in the synagogue with the Jews, - - and in the market place daily with them that met with him. Then certain philosophers of the Epicureans and of the Stoics, encountered him. Some said, What will this babbler say? Others, He seemeth to be a setter forth of strange gods: because he preached to them <u>Jesus, and the resurrection</u>."*
> (Acts 17:16-18)

> *"-- But God commandeth all men everywhere to repent, Because he hath appointed a day, in which he will judge the world in righteousness by that man whom he hath ordained: concerning*

> *which he hath given assurance unto all men, in that <u>he hath raised him from the dead</u>. And when they heard of the resurrection of the dead, some mocked: and others said, We will hear thee again on this matter." (Acts 17:30-32).*

There is only one gospel that is effective today in this the church age, and that is the gospel that the Apostle Paul gave us, the gospel of salvation. If we desire to see souls saved and we become what Jesus promised when He said "I will make you become fishers of men" (Mk. 1:17), then we are obliged to follow the formula He gave for success.

> *"For I am not ashamed of the gospel of Christ; for it is the power of God unto salvation to everyone that believeth; to the Jew first, and also to the Greek." (Ro. 1:16)*

After the Church is completed and is raptured into the Lord's presence, the Gospel of salvation will no longer be the dominant message of God to men. There is another gospel mentioned in Scripture that seems to be an interim gospel that fills the void that exists between that which was preached during the church age and that which will be proclaimed during the kingdom age. This is the same period in which the momentous events of the "tribulation" take place. The Apostle John writes,

> *"And I saw another angel fly in the midst of heaven, having the everlasting gospel to preach unto them that dwell on the earth, and to every nation, and kindred, and tongue, and people, saying with a loud voice, Fear God, and give glory to him; for the hour of judgment is come; --" (Rev. 14:6-7).*

This gospel, called the "Everlasting Gospel," is preached by an angel. The Church has just recently been raptured away, and for a brief period of time there is not a single believer left on earth. The message is quite simple; fear God, give glory to Him, judgment is come. It is a very effective message for an extremely difficult time. This message is similar to the one that Jonah brought and delivered to Nineveh, (Jonah 3:4) and it had similar results. Again, turning to the Scriptures, we are told of the outcome of this angelic preaching,

> *"After this I beheld and lo, a great multitude, which no man could number, of all nations, -- stood before the throne, and before the Lamb, -- These are they who came out of (the great) tribulation, and have washed their robes, and made them white in the blood of the Lamb." (Rev. 7:9, 14).*

Angels are powerful, majestic, creatures, certainly of a superior order than that of fallen, sinfull, natural man. They are creatures that are familiar with the environs of heaven and of the presence of the living God. Men do not fail to give them due attention and respect at their rare appearances on earth. Imagine! An angel in midair preaching to men. Incredible! The use of an angel in this instance reveals the urgency of the situation. God employs a method that would surely catch the attention of earth dwellers. The appearance of this heavenly being would unfailingly leave an indelible impression upon all men who see and hear him.

The message he brings is gospel (good news) all right, but it is not the "gospel of salvation" of the church age. The content of this gospel that the angel brings seems to be summed up in three parts. 1) God is Sovereign; 2) God is Judge; and 3) God is Creator. This fits very well with what the Apostle Paul wrote in Romans chapter one about the responsibility of all men everywhere.

> *"For the wrath of God is revealed from heaven against all ungodliness and unrighteousness of men, who hold the truth in unrighteousness, because that which may be known of God is manifest in them; for God hath shown it unto them. For the invisible things of him from the creation of the world are clearly seen, being understood by the things that are made, even his eternal power and Godhead, so that they are without excuse;" (Ro. 1:18-20).*

Once this dreadful time of tribulation is past, the attention of men will again be focused on the coming of the King and the setting up of the Millennial Kingdom as it was predicted by the prophets of the Old Testament. The gospel of the kingdom will again be the prevailing gospel as it was during the time of the Lord's first advent on earth. The Millennial Kingdom will be a one-world government with the LORD

Himself being the Sovereign on the throne. The Scriptures say, "This gospel of the kingdom shall be preached in all the world for a witness unto all nations; and then shall the end come." (Matt. 24:14). With Jesus seated on the throne and all nations, world wide, made subject to Him, it is not difficult to understand that over a thousand year period of time the gospel of the kingdom would be preached to every nation and every people.

Somewhat more complex is the statement that after the disclosure of this gospel to all nations that the end would come. It might be pertinent to ask, what end? Men have projected many different ideas, theories, as answers to this question but all of men's ideas have proven to be false. They have predicted the abrupt end of the world. Some predict the end of the human race, and some predict the end of all life. God is the only One who knows the future and He has promised eternal life to as many as obey Him and receive His Son as their Redeemer. Of even greater comfort and assurance is God's gift of the Holy Spirit to every believer in this present age and with Him comes the promise that He will <u>never</u> leave us. Jesus said, "I go to prepare a place for you. And if I go and prepare a place for you, I will come again, and receive you unto myself, that where I am, there ye may be also." (Jn. 14:2-3).

It seems rather obvious that neither the believer nor the Church was in view when Jesus spoke of the end. What then was the end the Lord was referring to? The answer to that question can best be found in the book of Revelation. When the 1000 year kingdom has run its course there is a final rebellion by man which is quickly and violently quelled by God. (Rev. 20:7-9). This marks the end of sin as rebellion. It also marks the end of Satan's freedom and activity. (Rev. 20:10). The prophecy in Revelation then says that creation as we know it comes to an end.

> *"And I saw a great white throne, and him that sat on it, from whose face the earth and the heavens fled away, and there was found no place for them. (Rev. 20:11). And I saw a new heaven and a new earth; for the first heaven and the first earth were passed away, and there was no more sea." (Rev. 21:1).*

*Chapter 5*

The old world gone -- completely done away and in its place a new earth -- a new home for the righteous. With every thing new, man passes into eternity and there is an end to time. This is incredible! Men are prone to say "How can these things be?" God being GOD, The Sovereign One, The Omnipotent, can do as He pleases and this is the way He says it will be.

*Chapter VI*

## THE MYSTERY OF HIS WILL

*"Having made known unto us the mystery of his will, according to his good pleasure which he has purposed in himself."*
*(Eph. 1:9).*

God's will: What a wonderful thing to know. Of all the mysteries, this one brings the deepest sense of peace and satisfaction to my own soul. How good of God to reveal these great truths to us that we might know where we stand in His plan and program. Jesus said "You shall know the truth and the truth shall make you free." (Jn. 8:32). Free from doubt, fear, condemnation; freedom to glory in our standing before Him as true sons and heirs. Free! What a wonderful word -- a word chucked full of favorable potentials. Men have fought and died for their conception of what they believe to be the meaning of this little word. Jesus said "the truth shall set you free", and He went on to say "-- all things that I have heard of my Father I have made known unto you." This word of God, the Bible, is known and available to most men in western cultures. Down through the centuries the Church has grown and multiplied as men found the Bible to be true, and they discovered the freedom that Jesus spoke of and promised. I am speaking of spiritual, mental, and emotional freedom which is of more importance to the individual than physical or political freedom. Some have spent their entire lives as slaves or prisoners and yet have had mental freedom. These same people may attain a certain amount of contentment, satisfaction, even joy in their lives despite the fact of being physically confined. In contrast, the person who is mentally depressed, without hope for the future, carrying a load of guilt, and fearful of death, is usually a person who is miserable, desperate, and brought right up to the point of being suicidal. The rate of suicide today, especially among younger persons is startling, and indicates a sense of hopelessness, or a lack of perceived freedom and mental peace.

Many times I have had different individuals come to me and say "I wish I knew God's will for me." Usually I understand this statement to refer to the short term, the will of God for a person's life which has to do with the immediate present or at least with the immediate future. When looking at "the mystery of God's will" we must look at the big picture -- the over all long range view of God's purpose for the individual. Now it is true if we are able see the outer perimeter or the extremities of His will, it becomes much easier for us to determine the direction and the application of the short term or the present will of God for us.

In the sixth chapter of the gospel of John, there are eight times between verses thirty seven and fifty four that we find the proclamation "I will" or its equivalent is used by the Lord. On four of the occasions, when concerning the believer as a child of God, the Word says, "<u>I will</u> raise him up at the last day". In this passage our Savior is giving extraordinary emphasis to this truth of resurrection. He has repeated the assertion many times; it is of great importance. Let us take care that we do not miss it. This is the heart, the center, of the teaching on the "blessed hope" that is the basis for the steadfastness for every believer. The author of Hebrews writes of this hope "as an anchor of the soul, both sure and steadfast --" (Heb. 6:19). In the present era it is important for every believer to have an anchor for one's soul. This is an age in which many trends and movements have done a great deal to remove all absolutes from life. Many increasingly find themselves adrift in a slough of relativity. It is only in God and His word that moral stability is found, with accompanying hope and safety. God has spoken, and either His word is true and can be relied upon or He is a liar. People of all ages, past and present, give witness to the fact that God is able to do all that He has promised. This witness comes in the form of changed lives of men in every imaginable situation. It was well stated when a man said "God has spoken, I believe it, that settles it." This is the kind of commitment God is looking for in the life of every person.

*Chapter 6*

In Jesus' High Priestly prayer recorded in the seventeenth chapter of John's gospel, the Savior expresses His own will only once when He says "Father, I will that they also, whom thou hast given me, be with me where I am, that they may behold my glory, which thou hast given me, for thou lovedst me before the foundation of the world." (vs. 24).

Just before the above cited text, while speaking on the subject of His followers, Jesus said, "For I have given unto them the words which thou gavest me, and they have received them, and have known that I came out from thee, and they have believed that thou didst send me. I pray for them; I pray not for the world, but for them whom thou hast given me; for they are thine." (Jn. 17:8-9). To know that in His past ministry here on earth, Jesus prayed for us, and is continuing to do so in His present ministry as an advocate before the Father, gives the believer grounds for an immense source of assurance. As Hebrew's says, "Wherefore, He is able to save them to the uttermost that come unto God by Him, seeing He ever liveth to make intercession for them" (Heb. 7:25). It is well to note in passing this way, that all Jesus work in this era is in behalf of believers. In His prayer He said, "I pray not for the world." His work for the world of unsaved men ended in His death on the cross. He closed this chapter of His ministry when He said just before He died, "It is finished." All that He could do for sinners had been done, now it was up to them to believe and receive life or perish.

The text of the theme "the mystery of his will" is given in twelve verses, from verse three through verse fourteen of the first chapter of the Epistle to the Ephesians. It begins with the declaration that believers are blessed with all Spiritual blessings. The text goes on to say, all the while using the past tense, that He 1) <u>HAS</u> made us accepted in Christ, 2) we <u>HAVE</u> redemption through His blood, 3) we <u>HAVE</u> the forgiveness of sins. These are blessings each and every believer possesses here and now; they are not things to strive for and hope to obtain at some future date. Volumes could be, and have been, written on each of these blessings, as men of God have caught the truth of what the Bible is here disclosing to the church.

Listed above are but three of a long register of blessings that God has prepared and freely given to every believer who is "in Christ." And yet these blessings tell of only one side of the whole picture. The Bible says, "Blessed is the man to whom the Lord will not impute sin." (Ro. 4:8). The word "impute" means "to charge to" or "to attribute to". Blessed is that individual to whom God will not charge with sin. And why not? Because sin, <u>ALL</u> sin, has been relegated to Christ, who took it upon Himself in His death, and thus paid the account for sin in full. Christ died in our place, for our sin. The Bible says that our sin was imputed to Christ and that in turn His righteousness is imputed to us. This is a classic case of substitution. "He made him who knew no sin to be sin on our behalf, that we might become the righteousness of God in him." (II Cor. 5:21). NASB

The average Christian, speaking only of those who have experienced regeneration, has not fully and properly conceived, much less appreciated, just how blessed of God he really is. Most Christians, just like Paul in Romans chapter seven, go stumbling and blundering along in this life and they cry as he did, "Oh wretched man that I am." There is no need for this; God has prepared something better and He is the One who said "blessed is the man".

We would be remiss if we overlooked another facet of God's will for the believer. This one is found in the book of First Corinthians and is also from Paul's pen.

> *"There hath no temptation taken you but such as is common to man; but God is faithful, who <u>will not</u> permit you to be tempted above that ye are able, but <u>will,</u> with the temptation, also make the way to escape, that ye may be able to bear it."*
> *(I Cor. 10:13).*

Not only will God not charge sin against those who believe in Him, but He goes a step further by saying that He will not even permit us to be tempted to sin above our ability to cope. This is due to the presence of the Holy Spirit within each believer, who will give the strength and the direction to proceed, to avoid succumbing to those things which would shatter fellowship with the Lord. The ability to avoid succumbing to temptation requires taking several steps on the part of the believer. First, there must be a recognition of the temptation and a placing of it before God through prayer. Secondly, there must be a strong de-

Chapter 6

sire to act in obedience to God's Word, and a stiffening or steeling of one's own will to resolve to remain obedient.. This is what Ephesians chapter four and Colossians chapter three are all about. It is there we read,

> "That <u>ye put off</u> concerning the former manner of life the old man, which is corrupt - - And that <u>ye put on</u> the new man which after God is created in righteousness and true holiness. Wherefore, putting away lying, speak every man truth - - Let no corrupt communication proceed out of your mouth, but that which is good to the use of edifying, that it may minister grace unto the hearers." (Eph. 4:24-25, 29).

It is very clear in these passages of Scripture that there is a definite part that every Christian must play in mastering iniquities in his daily activities and gaining victory over sins. These verses lay out stringent guidelines and distinct commands to the child of God, and we must act accordingly if we are to expect victory and blessing. God has and will continue to do for the Christian that which he could not do for himself, and yet, at the same time, He will not do those things which He has commanded us to do. We must do our part if He is to be true in doing His. The chapter in Colossians reads,

> "<u>But now ye also put off</u> all these: anger, wrath, malice, blasphemy, filthy communication -- Lie not one to another, seeing that <u>ye have put off</u> the old man with his deeds, And <u>(you) have put on</u> the new man that is renewed in knowledge after the image of him that created him; -- <u>(you) put on</u>, therefore, as the elect of God, holy and beloved, -- And above all these things put on love, --" (Col. 3:8-10, 12, 14).

We have examined the first two steps in breaking the power of temptation; the third step is perhaps the most important of all. This step entails the concept of filling the mind with thoughts other than those which tempt. A man may not have much control over the thoughts that pop into his mind, but he does have control of how long these thoughts stay there in his mind. A good habit for the Christian to develop in times of temptation is that of replacing the evil thoughts with a passage of Scripture. This is an excellent time to concentrate on memorizing key verses.

*"Thy word have I hid in mine heart, that I might not sin against thee." (Psa. 119:11).*

The believer should just let the Word saturate his mind and his heart. The key to victory is the Word of God. The more we think on Scriptural things the more the Scripture will replace the destructive thoughts of temptation.

*"Speaking to yourselves in psalms and hymns and spiritual songs, singing and making melody in your hearts to the Lord." (Eph. 5:19).*

*"Finally, brethern, whatever things are true, whatever things are honest, whatever things are just, whatever things are pure, whatever things are lovely, whatever things are of good report; if there be any virtue, and if there be any praise, <u>think on these things</u>" (Phil. 4:8).*

To a great extent faith is built around the promises that God gives in His Word, and the more fully that we understand the promises the greater and stronger our faith will be. The Apostle Peter gives strong testimony to this truth by saying to those who "have obtained like precious faith,"

*"Grace and peace be multiplied unto you through the <u>KNOWLEDGE</u> of God and of Jesus, our Lord, according as divine power hath given unto us all things that pertain unto life and godliness, through the <u>KNOWLEDGE</u> of him that hath called us to glory and virtue; by which are given unto us exceeding great and precious promises, that by these ye might be partakers of the divine nature, having escaped the corruption that is in the world through lust." (II Pet. 1:2-4).*

Two of these "great and precious promises" are found in the teaching of the subjects of "adoption" and its closely related partner "predestination". There is a good deal of fear and apprehension generated in some Christian quarters when these subjects are discussed. Many Christians have been led to believe that these doctrines are beyond their spiritual understanding, and that they are better left in the classrooms of Bible colleges and seminaries. Satan does his best to both perpetrate and to perpetuate this belief, and thus destroy the source of so much comfort and assurance the Lord has provided for daily Christian living.

It is my purpose to show that with the proper comprehension and spiritual insight, these truths can be of great significance and comfort to the average Christian. Because these twin doctrines - adoption and predestination - are Bible subjects, we can expect the Holy Spirit to graciously and truthfully open their meaning to our understanding that we may receive practical help for daily living.

## *ADOPTION*

We will begin by looking at two verses from Paul's letter to the church in Rome that are very pertinent to the subject of adoption. Both are located in the eighth chapter. First, Paul says,

*"For ye have not received the spirit of bondage again to fear; but ye have received the Spirit of adoption, whereby we cry, Abba, Father." (Ro. 8:15)*

*"And not only they, but ourselves also, who have the first fruits of the Spirit, even we ourselves groan within ourselves, <u>waiting</u> for the adoption, that is, the redemption of our body." (Ro. 8:23).*

For the Christian, membership in the family of God comes about by birth and not by adoption as is sometimes taught. As we have seen in former chapters of this study, Jesus said "ye must be born again," and it is through this new and Spiritual birth that we become sons of God. The Apostle John, when writing his letters, frequently used the term "my little children" (I Jn. 2:1,18; 3:2), which in the original Greek is the word "teknon" literally meaning "born ones." There is no conflict of truth between the idea of the believer's new birth and the adoption spoken of in Romans 8:23 which says that we are still "waiting for the adoption." The truth is that adoption is yet future for every born again believer because it takes place at the time of the redemption of the believer's body. Thus, the adoption takes place among the events that accompany the rapture -- that time when all believers (the true church) are "caught up" to be with their Lord.

Because the English language lacks a word containing the exact meaning of the word used in the Greek, "huio thesia", the translators of the English bible used the word "adoption" as that with the nearest, most accurate rendering. According to Webster's Third New International Dictionary, adoption means "the taking of an outsider into a family by investing him with the rights and responsibilities of a member by birth." When an adoption takes place, a person, born of other parents, is legally <u>MADE</u> a member of a family with all the resulting attachments. In contrast to this, the dictionary section of Strong's Exhaustive Concordance of the Bible, gives the meaning of the Greek words "huio thesia" as the "<u>PLACING</u>" of a son.

There can be little doubt that the word adoption is used in two somewhat different shades of meaning in the book of Romans as it is being reviewed. In the eighth chapter as seen above, the word is used concerning every single individual member who is in the composition of the body of The Church, The Bride of Christ. This is in some contrast to the use of the word adoption in the ninth chapter, as the author Paul turns his (and the reader's) attention away from individual believers and directs it toward the nation of Israel. To quote from (Romans 9:4-5),

*"Who are Israelites; to whom pertaineth the ADOPTION, and the glory, and the covenants, and the giving of the law, and the service of God, and the promises; Whose are the fathers, and of whom, as concerning the flesh, Christ came, who is over all, God blessed forever. Amen"  (Ro. 9:4-5).*

The adoption as used here pertains to the national entity of the nation Israel and not to separate individuals. Israel was placed as a singular nation in a particular place and time to fulfill a special purpose. This is what God said of that nation through His servants Moses and Hosea,

> *"For thou art an holy people unto the Lord thy God, and the Lord hath chosen thee to be a peculiar people unto himself, above all the nations that are upon the earth." (Deu. 14:2).*

> *"When Israel was a child, then I loved him, and called my son out of Egypt" (Hosea 11:1).*

God took an existing nation and "placed" it in a very unique position, one that no other nation has ever occupied, nor ever will. He called Israel His "firstborn" (Ex. 4:22) and went even further in His expression of love by calling that nation "the apple of His eye." God, in His sovereignty, elevated Israel to this lofty position, and He has never rescinded His order or changed His mind. God's love is immutable, it never varies or fails. This is one use of the word adoption in the New Testament, but there is another that is far more meaningful to the believer today.

In our society today, a child born to a family is a son and an heir with many rights and privileges. But even having been born a son, there are many things that are withheld or denied him. Our law declares him to be a minor until the age of twenty one, and being a minor he is under the authority of his parents. Until he comes of age there are many legal things he cannot do, such as vote, get a driver's license, marry a wife, borrow money, enter into a contract, purchase liquor, etc. Due to the stresses of modern society some states have eased some restrictions and have allocated certain privileges prior to age twenty one -- even to as young as sixteen. Nevertheless, the principal remains that one can be born a son and still be restricted as to rights and responsibilities. Once the individual has attained his majority at the legal age of twenty one, he then enjoys all the legal rights available to any and all members of the family. He is then considered to be a mature, full grown, adult son.

Paul's teaching on the subject of adoption finds a meaningful parallel in modern society. We are born into the family of God at the moment of salvation, but we are still spiritual babes, mere toddlers in God's kingdom. Paul delineates this truth in his letter written to the Galatians when he says, "For ye are all the sons of God by faith in Christ Jesus" (Gal. 3:26), a little later he adds,

> *"Now I say that the heir, as long as he is a child, differeth nothing from a servant, though he be lord of all, but is under tutors and governors until the time appointed of the father. Even so we, when we were children, were in bondage under the elements of the world. But, when the fullness of the time was come, God sent forth his Son, made of a woman, made under the law, to redeem them that were under the law, that we might receive the adoption of sons." (Gal. 4:1-5).*

These verses further show, just as we have seen, that an heir, as long as he is a child, is in a position little different from that of a servant. He must be obedient to his parents, teachers, instructors, and to all those in positions of authority until an appointed time. After establishing this fact, Paul changes from illustration to application and gives a truth of paramount importance. The passage quoted above shows that from the very beginning God's purpose was to make believers "to be like Christ." Verses 4 and 5 say that God sent His Son for a specific designated intention - - to redeem them that were under the law, and this redemption is also for a definite purpose . The Scriptures clearly say that we are redeemed that we might receive the "adoption." Notice that in the fifth verse Paul uses the word "we", thus including himself in the subject group. Then, regarding this group, he goes on to say "that we might receive the adoption of sons", an event he was anticipating as a future occurrence. We do not attain full rights nor the "<u>placement</u>" as sons until our salvation is final and the redemption of the body is complete. Again notice how Paul says in Romans 8:23 that we are "waiting for the adoption" which is "the redemption of the body." This adoption should be thought of as a climactic height, the complete actualization of a truth that should captivate our minds and hearts.

> *"For as many as are led by the Spirit of God, they are the sons of God. For ye have not received the spirit of bondage again to fear; but ye have received the Spirit of adoption, whereby we cry, Abba, Father. The Spirit Himself beareth witness with our*

*spirit that we are the children of God; and if children, then heirs -- heirs of God, and joint heirs with Christ -- if so be that we suffer with him, that we may be also glorified together. For I reckon that the sufferings of this present time are not worthy to be compared with the glory which shall be revealed in us. For the earnest expectation of the creation waiteth for the manifestation of the sons of God. For the creation was made subject to vanity, not willingly but by reason of him who hath subjected the same in hope. Because the creation itself also shall be delivered from the bondage of corruption into the glorious liberty of the children of God. For we know that the whole creation groaneth and travaileth in pain together until now. And not only they, but ourselves also, who have the first fruits of the Spirit even we ourselves groan within ourselves, <u>waiting for the adoption</u>, that is, the redemption of our body." (Ro. 8:14-23).*

Let us enumerate the truths of this quoted passage. 1) Believers here and now are recognized to be the sons of God. (v 14); 2) The Holy Spirit Himself is witness to this truth of our being the children of God. (v 16); 3) Because we are sons of God we are heirs -- meaning we have an inheritance. (v 17); 4) Part of the inheritance we are to receive is to be glorified, which means our redemption will be completed, and we will have immortality with corresponding honor, dignity, and reputation. (vs 17-18); 5) The whole creation is waiting in expectancy for this unveiling of believers in their glorified bodies that God has promised. (v 19); 6) Creation itself will share in the blessing of the occasion, as it is liberated from bondage of the curse given in Genesis 3:18. (v 19); and 7) This, the moment of glorification for the believer, is also the time when each will be "placed" (exposed) in full adoption as children of God for all creation to see.

These verses also tell us of spiritual benefits which we may currently enjoy. The Scripture says that we HAVE "the first fruits of the Spirit" and this leads to the obvious question -- what are they? These "first fruits" are the immediate possessions of every believer -- forgiveness, redemption, justification, security, and sanctification. Adoption is not listed here, since for believers adoption will be one of the final fruits of the Spirit. Of special comfort to those who believe, is the promise that even NOW we have been granted the "Spirit of adoption" who is really the Holy Spirit Himself. Carefully observe that the passage does not say that we have the adoption itself, but rather we have the Spirit that will bring about the adoption. In providing "so great salvation" God, in His wisdom, gave the indwelling Holy Spirit as the guarantee to the individual believer, that what He had begun He would surely finish. It is to be understood that while adoption has not yet been experienced by the believer, he has received the Spirit from God Who will accomplish this much anticipated event in its proper time.

> *"Beloved, now are we the sons of God, and it doth not yet appear what we shall be, but we know that, when he shall appear, we shall be like him; for we shall see him as he is." (I Jn. 3:2).*

Before leaving this subject of adoption, there is a passage in Matthew's gospel which should attract our attention. Jesus is illuminating truth to His disciples through the use of parables, and the truth being exposed is relevant to the topic under discussion.

> *"So shall it be in the end of this age. The Son of Man shall send forth his angels, and they shall gather out of his kingdom all things that offend, and them who do iniquity, and shall cast them into a furnace of fire; there shall be wailing and gnashing of teeth. Then shall the righteous shine forth as the sun in the kingdom of their Father. Who hath ears, let him hear.*
> *(Matt. 13:40-43).*

The Lord says the things referred to take place at the end of the age -- signifying they are yet future. Then, in this future time, the righteous (believers) will shine like the sun. This is the same expression used in Matthew 17:2 when speaking of the Lord Himself during His transfiguration experience. The Lord in His glorified state is dazzling bright, and Christians -- after receiving their glorified bodies -- will be like Him.

## PREDESTINATION

*"For whom he did foreknow, he also did predestinate to be conformed to the image of his Son, that he might be the first born among many brethren." (Ro. 8:29).*

*"Moreover, whom he did predestinate, them he also called; and whom he called, them he also justified; and whom he justified, them he also glorified." (Ro. 8:30).*

*"Having predestinated us unto the adoption of sons by Jesus Christ to himself, according to the good pleasure of his will," (Eph. 1:5).*

*"In whom also we have obtained an inheritance, being predestinated according to the purpose of him who worketh all things after the counsel of his own will." (Eph. 1:11).*

Biblical teaching concerning predestination is inextricably linked to, and should never be separated from, the teaching about adoption. The two go hand in hand and to separate them is to open the door to error. The Bible says in Ephesians 1:5 that all members of the true Church, which is the body of which Christ is the head, are "predestined to be conformed to the image of his Son." This is the central truth that constitutes the "blessed hope" of every believer. We are to be -- will be -- like Christ.

There are those who associate and apply predestination with salvation but I believe this view is mistaken. There are only four references to predestination found in the New Testament -- two are in the book of Romans and two in the book of Ephesians -- and all four show the essential link to be with adoption and inheritance; NOT with salvation. Predestination concerns ONLY believers, those who know Jesus Christ as Savior, and has nothing to do with the unsaved. There are those who believe and teach that some people are predestined to be saved, and thus are then forced to take the position that other people are predestined to be lost. However, this is a wholly untenable situation in the light of many passages of Scripture. To take one example, we read in II Peter 3:8 that "God is NOT WILLING that any should perish but that all should come to repentance." For one to believe that people -- adults, children, or even new born infants, that God has predestined to an eternity in hell is absolutely ludicrous. I can find no scriptural support for such a position and believe it is a mistaken conception taken from the mind of men rather than a revelation from the mind of God.

Next lets examine the etymology of the word predestination and see how our understanding of this term can be embellished. The first syllable "pre" means "earlier than" or "beforehand", and the larger word "destination" means terminus or the farthest extent. When the two are put together there emerges the meaning that beforehand the final destination or objective is determined or known. An important point to make at this juncture is that there is no concept intrinsic to the word that suggests anything to do with events that might occur between the beginning and the predefined ending. In other words, the end or culmination is prefigured but not particular circumstances prior to and along the way to the end. A good illustration of the principle involved is that of an individual who purchases a bus ticket, the acquisition of which represents a contract that implies that the person will be delivered to the agreed upon city of his chosen destination. The agreement says nothing concerning events between the departure and the arrival. There may be mechanical failures, flat tires, bridges out, detours, alternate routes, delays, -- innumerable possibilities -- but the agreement is that the passenger will be delivered to his destination.

Now let us pass from illustration to experience. God has a master plan that He has worked out that provides everything that could possibly be required for man's salvation from sin and his sanctification to sonship. It was a perfect and complete plan before God ever began to execute it. In this plan it was determined that Jesus Christ, God's own Son, would offer His own life for the price of redemption for man from the penalty of sin. This is the reason why in the book of Revelation 13:8, the Apostle John speaks of Jesus as "the Lamb slain from the foundation of the world." The Apostle Peter emphasizes this same truth when he wrote,

# Chapter 6

*"But with the precious blood of Christ, as of a lamb without blemish and without spot, who verily was foreordained before the foundation of the world." (I Pet. 1:19-20).*

There is a strong emphasis here that these things were all parts of a program planned by God even before creation. In this plan it was resolved that if anyone by his or her own choice would accept Jesus Christ as Savior, this person would then have but one ending or terminus -- not only to be WITH Christ but also to be LIKE Him. According to Jesus' teaching in Matthew 7:14, when one passes through the strait gate and begins the journey up the narrow way that describes the path that those who follow Him must tread, there is only one end; it is clearly established that the road leads to eternal life as a son of God, nowhere else.

Life's experiences for the Christian are at least as varied and difficult as for other men. The Christian's daily walk may include the entire range of experiences from times of great blessing and happiness, to those of danger, hardship, disappointment, and failure. But through it all the Christian has something going for him that others do not. He knows -- or should know -- that he is predestined -- that in the end he will be what God intends him to be, LIKE CHRIST.

In my own experience, I'm somewhere between the "pre" of what God has beforehand promised, and the "destination" which will be the end or finished product He plans me to be. I have been saved for more than forty years, but I have not arrived at the terminus of this experience. I am not yet what God has purposed for me to become.

## Chapter VII

# THE MYSTERY OF THE FAITH

*Faith is the one means at our disposal of possessing all the benefits that God has provided for the Christian and for the Church.*

*"--- Holding the mystery of the faith in a pure conscience"* (I Tim. 3:9).

*"Beloved, when I gave all diligence to write unto you of the common salvation, it was needful for me to write unto you, and exhort you that ye should earnestly contend for the faith which was once delivered unto the saints." (Jude 1:3).*

Faith itself does not need to be a great mystery, for by it men of all ages past and present are saved. Nevertheless, faith is a many-faceted reality and can be a complex concept to understand. There are a number of different dictionary definitions of the word "faith" among which are the following:

1) confidence in a person, statement, or thing as being trustworthy.

2) belief without certain proof.

3) belief in God as recorded in the Scriptures.

4) A system of religious belief. i.e., the Christian faith

5) anything given adherence or credence. i.e., political faith

6) allegiance or fidelity.

In the light of these definitions we may conclude that biblical or spiritual faith is a personal confidence in God. This confidence is a reliance upon a God who is believed to be trustworthy. Faith is the act by which men lay hold of and appropriate the truths of the gospel of salvation, and rely on the work done by Christ in their stead to secure that salvation for them. Saving faith, while being a one-time occurrence, denotes three separate actions in the minds of men. These three are 1) a conviction of the understanding, 2) an assent of the will, and 3) a trust of the heart.

*"Let us draw near with a true heart in full assurance of faith, - -- Let us hold fast the profession of our faith without wavering [for he is faithful that promised],---"* (Heb. 10:22-23).

We are not talking about the subject of faith in some vague or general sense, but rather particularly of faith in God or even more specifically, faith in the Word of God. The first, or most elementary, level of faith leading to a knowledge of God requires a faith in His Word. As Paul wrote, "So faith cometh by hearing, and hearing by the Word of God." (Rom. 10:17). Furthermore Jesus said,

*"All things are delivered unto me by my Father, and no man knoweth the Son, but the Father; neither knoweth any man the Father, except the Son, and he to whomsoever the Son will reveal him."* (Matt. 11:27).

Faith in God's Word leads to knowledge of Jesus, God's Son, and faith in Jesus leads to knowledge of God the Father.

Faith <u>MUST</u> be moored by something, and biblical faith is secured by the Word of God. This aspect of faith bears upon the theme of our study of New Testament mysteries because faith in God's Word, the "gospel of salvation," is necessary in order to understand the mystery it speaks of. Faith is only as powerful as its object. If indeed the object of faith is the Pauline gospel of salvation by regeneration then that faith is on firm footing. Most all civil governments have their laws based on Biblical morality. The term most often used of these governments is that they are based on Christian/Judeo ethics. More and more nations are experiencing a trend toward what is called personal rights or personal freedom. The rights of a person taking precedent over the rights of society as a whole. As the pendulum swings in that direction and laws are passed expediting the trend, we are seeing society change rapidly away from Biblical morality to that of an amoral state. This is a time when it is not considered to be "politically correct" to stand on high Christian morals that have been in effect for centuries. Nevertheless, the type of faith that provides a real anchor in times of great stress, is based on the never failing, ever appropriate Word of God. It has been said, "God answers prayer of genuine faith, NOT prayers of positive thinking." Many people think that if they just believe hard enough they can cause God to move or act. I call that having faith in faith. All evidence points to the conclusion this does not work.

The Bible clearly shows there are two distinct views of the subject of faith. As we have just seen, there is the one time experience of saving faith, when an individual who realizes he is a guilty and condemned rebel before God, takes the opportunity of repentance and accepts Christ's saving work and passes from death to life. It is at the moment of such a decision that a spiritual new birth occurs and the individual becomes a "child of God." The term "child of God" is used here with a particular meaning. There is never a birth of any sort when the newly born is not considered a baby. An infant is one without experience, knowledge, or understanding. The Holy Spirit gave sound instruction through the Apostle Peter on this very issue when he wrote: "As newborn babes, desire the sincere milk of the Word, that ye may grow by it, if so be ye have tasted that the Lord is gracious." (I Pet. 2:2-3). Peter then further added "But grow in grace, and in the knowledge of our Lord and Savior, Jesus Christ." (II Pet. 3:18).

At this stage in the life of the new "believer" the second aspect of faith begins to operate. As the new Christian begins to grow he does so by feeding on the Word of God. As he develops in knowledge and understanding of the Word he matures as a Christian. In the book of Hebrews chapter five, it speaks of one who fails to grow or mature in his or her Christian experience, for there it says:

*"For when for the time ye ought to be teachers, ye have need that one teach you again the first principles of the oracles of*

*God, and are become such as have need of milk, and not of [solid food]. For everyone that useth milk is unskillful in the word of righteousness; for he is a babe. But [solid food] belongeth to them that are of full age, even those who by reason of use have their senses exercised to discern both good and evil".* (Heb. 5:12-14).

This is not a contradiction of that which Peter wrote but rather reveals there is a natural growth or progression in the spiritual life of the believer. One passes through the stage of being a babe or child and enters the area of a young adult and continues on to full maturity. One of the tragedies of life is to see an individual grow to adulthood physically but mentally remain undeveloped. For this to happen in the spiritual arena is equally tragic and is the very essence for the reason the author of the book of Hebrews finds it necessary to give the warning that he does. Unlike the mentally retarded, though, the spiritually undeveloped person does not get help from the society in which he lives. The truth is that society rarely if ever recognizes the problem. In fact it is society, of which we are an intricate part, that contributes greatly to spiritual underdevelopment; "the world" is constantly throwing up roadblocks and hindrances to spiritual well being. If the "babe in Christ" does not get help from the local church or from close Christian friends he may very likely not develop into a mature Christian.

In Gal. 5:22 faith is listed seventh in the various forms of "the fruit of the Spirit" which means that it is something to be desired and garnered in the life of every believer. Faith is the application of God's Word into the process of daily living. Practically every "believer" knows more of God's Word than what he actually applies in his day by day experience. This is where living by faith should occur, as more and more Godly precepts are put into practice, and a maturation takes place. The Bible teaches very positively that our faith must be centered on God's Word. It goes on to say "Now faith is the substance of things hoped for, the evidence of things not seen." (Heb. 11:1). Faith always has substance and evidence. Substance speaks of the real nature of a thing in its essential elements and chief characteristics. Substance then, is the revealing of the characteristic components of any entity under study. Furthermore, having faith shows evidence of a clear perception of God's Word and of His ways. Much of God's promised program is as yet unfulfilled, but for the believer, the eye of faith sees the outline of God's whole plan and this is sufficient evidence to readily accept the entire package. Faith is never blind. Speaking of believers of the past, the Bible says,

> *"These all died in faith, not having received the promises but having seen them afar off, and were persuaded of them, and embraced them, and confessed that they were strangers and pilgrims on the earth." (Heb. 11:13).*

From the Bible's standpoint, there is no such thing as a real faith that is blind. True faith <u>always</u> has God's Word to back it up. One's faith is only as solid as one's knowledge or understanding of the Word of God. The more a believer knows of God's Word the more faith he can exercise. When a personal holy walk before the Lord is desired (as it should be) the Bible indicates that knowledge of God's Word is the key to success. "Thy Word have I hid in my heart, that I might not sin against thee." (Psa. 119:11). Knowledge of the Word is also imperative for the established Christian who is walking with his Lord; he cannot maintain his mature status or hope to advance it, or do the Lord's will in the world, unless he continues to learn of the Word.

*Chapter VIII*

# THE MYSTERY OF THE IN-LIVING CHRIST

*"For it is God who worketh <u>in you</u> both to will and to do of his good pleasure." (Phil. 2:13).*

*"-- Of which I am made a minister, according to the dispensation of God which is given to me for you, to fulfill the word of God, Even the mystery which hath been hidden from ages and from generations, but now is made manifest to his saints, To whom God would make known what is the riches of the glory of this mystery among the Gentiles, which is <u>Christ in you</u>, the hope of glory; Whom we preach --" (Col. 1:25-28).*

The context in which this text from Colossians is taken runs from chapter 1:12 to 2:3. This context speaks of the glorious heavenly standing of the believer. Our present salvation is unto eternal life and involves an intimate association with the God of glory who is within Himself infinitely righteous. Because God is holy, He cannot accept anything less than perfection in man if the two are to have an intimate association. Fellowship with a Holy God requires a perfection far beyond human attainment, and thus a bestowed righteousness is the only righteousness which God will accept. We are justified before God only because we have been <u>declared</u> righteous through the meritorious work of Christ. We cannot enter into God's presence without receiving this imputed righteousness. The righteousness that is ascribed can only come about because of Jesus' resurrection from the dead. Christ's resurrection from the dead inaugurated a new creation, the beginnings of which can be obtained in the believer's spiritual life. The resurrected Jesus lives according to a new principle -- on a new plane of existence, if you will -- and His life after the resurrection is quite different from the one He lived before His death. His resurrection was not just a reversal of the death process. His body became a body such as was never seen before -- it was glorified. The Scriptures name it a "spiritual body." (I Cor. 15:44). Christ's resurrected state is one of perfect righteousness, perfectly balancing and connecting the body and spirit again as it was before sin came at the fall of Adam and Eve. This is the same type of body that is promised to every believer, for the New Testament says we will be new creatures, just like Him. (II Cor. 5:17). Our new body will be immortal, incorruptible, powerful, a glorious body; one truly fit for our regenerated spirit to dwell in. When we receive this new body, sometime yet future, then our salvation and sanctification will be complete. (See also chapter XII)

Today, when an individual becomes a believer in Christ, he immediately becomes a member of the mystical body of Christ, The Church. The Holy Spirit indwells each member and brings with Him eternal life. This life infuses every member and so the same life is found to be in every part of the body, including the Head, which is Christ. It is being placed in this mystical body that constitutes being "IN CHRIST." and all His merits are imputed to the believer. On this basis, and this basis alone, is a man justified before God. Many times I have envisioned myself as being encapsulated "in Christ" -- when God looks at me all He can see is His own Son and thus I am perfectly acceptable in His eyes. The Bible teaches that acceptance is based upon the merit of His Son, Jesus Christ, whose perfection is, through infinite grace, rendered available for every sinner.

In the study of the "mystery of the indwelling Christ" there comes to the forefront a beautiful parallel or complementary truth. The Epistle to the Ephesians tells of the blessings bestowed on the believer because he is "in Christ" while the Epistle to the Colossians reveals other blessings bestowed because Christ resides (indwells) in the believer. There is definitely two separate groups of benefits, blessings, for the believer to enjoy here and now in this life. If the first group, associated with being in Christ, is an accomplished reality, then the second group is sure to follow. On the subject of the believer's benefits in salvation there is a definite line of demarcation determined by these two different points of view. To be "in Christ" means to have been made the righteousness of God by which he is accepted forever in the Beloved. (See figure #5)

The expression "Christ in you" is properly referring to the indwelling Spirit of Christ, which is none other than the Holy Spirit. At the moment of regeneration the Holy Spirit takes up permanent residence in the life of each believer. Because He is a spirit, He can do this. Before His departure Jesus promised to send another Comforter as He knew our weaknesses, our need for direction, and our need for outside help. The coming of the Spirit was provision for every possible need that any believer might have in the progression through this life.

The believer is a new creation in Christ and concerning his position everything is changed from what he was. He is no longer one "having no hope, and without God in the world." (Eph. 2:12). In Christ, he is now forgiven, cleansed, and justified. The Bible gives needed assurance of this when it says "To the praise of the glory of his grace, through which he has made us accepted in the Beloved; In whom we have redemption through his blood, the forgiveness of sins, according to the riches of his grace, - - " (Eph. 1:6-7). The Holy Spirit has made His abode within the believer through the act of regeneration; His presence thus insuring eternal life and at the same time making the recipient a legal heir of God, joint heir with Christ. The believer is accepted in the Beloved forever. This is an indissoluble union. He has become a member of the mystical body of which Christ is the head. It is within this context of the believer being "in Christ," that is, in the mystical body, which is the True Church, that he enjoys the presence of the Holy Spirit dwelling in him. As a member of this body, each Christian has a place to fill with its attendant duties to perform that no other member can complete. Every member has been given one or more spiritual gifts to be used for a specific purpose. The Bible says these gifts are for

> *"the perfecting of the saints for the work of the ministry for the edifying of the body of Christ, till we all come in the unity of the faith, and of the knowledge of the Son of God, unto a perfect man, unto the measure of the stature of the fullness of Christ; that we henceforth be no more children, tossed to and fro, and*

*carried about by every wind of doctrine, -- but speaking the truth in love, may grow up into him in all things, who is the head, even Christ." (Eph. 4:12-15).*

The context in Colossians chapter one goes on to divulge the Son's preeminence: this in two divergent areas. First, He is said to be above all others in the task of creation; not only did He create all things but the passage then goes on to inform that all things were created <u>for</u> Him. Secondly, He is supreme in the work of redemption. There is no other who had the necessary ingredients to qualify for this high office of redeemer. Jesus alone filled the requirements and was willing to pay the full price exacted for man's sin.

Prior to Pentecost spoken of in the first two chapters of the book of Acts, regeneration was entirely unknown and unexperienced by men. Regeneration is the spiritual new birth that occurs when the Spirit of God enters the heart of man to indwell there. It is at this "new birth" that a man is born into the family of God and becomes an heir of God and a joint heir with Christ. The church, had its beginning on the day of Pentecost and every man that has received Christ as Savior and experienced the new birth has been added to the church since that day. No Old Testament saint ever experienced this regeneration and they know nothing of the glory and the blessing that belong to the church. The Scriptures relate many experiences where the Spirit of God came UPON an Old Testament saint but it never tells of their being indwelt. Significantly the Indwelling by the Spirit belongs to the church saint, and no other believer of any age has been blessed in a comparative way.

Jesus spoke to a Jewish ruler, Nicodemus, in a private, possibly furtive meeting, and spoke the words "Ye must be born again." (Jn. 3:7). Even though this man was a religious leader in the Jewish community and well versed in the then existing Scriptures, this saying by the Lord was completely baffling to him. Nothing like this had ever been taught before. Born again? What could it possibly mean? Nicodemus then asked Jesus if He was speaking of a feasible second physical birth and was told he was way off the mark. Jesus taught His disciples that He must soon leave them, but following His departure another Comforter would come to them and this new comforter would be non other than the Holy Spirit. Being a Spirit, and the Third Member of the Trinity, He would be able to bring about a spiritual new birth by indwelling each person who received Him. Thus the Scriptures say,

> *"And I will pray the Father, and he shall give you another Comforter, that he may abide with you forever; Even the Spirit of truth, whom the world cannot receive, because it seeth him not, neither knoweth him: but ye know him; for he dwelleth WITH you, and SHALL be IN you" (Jn. 14:16-17).*

Later the twelve disciples were instructed to wait in Jerusalem until they received the promised one.

> *"And, being assembled together with them, commanded them that they should not depart from Jerusalem, but wait for the promise of the Father, which, sayeth he, ye have heard from me" (Acts 1:4).*

## THE BELIEVER'S BENEFITS IN SALVATION

Different Perspectives from Different Views

| EPHESIANS | COLOSSIANS |
|---|---|
| (You) IN CHRIST | CHRIST IN YOU |
| Immediate Results | Long Term Results |
| SALVATION Eph. 2:13 | GOOD WORKS Phil. 1:6 |
| HEADSHIP II Cor. 5:17 | VICTORY I Jn. 4:4 |
| SECURITY | HOPE Col. 1:28 |

*"Now unto him who is able to do exceedingly abundantly above all that we ask or think, according to the <u>power that worketh in us</u>, --" (Eph. 3:20).*

Figure #5

## Chapter IX

# THE MYSTERY OF GODLINESS (PIETY)

Christ, the prime example of Godliness: being filled with reverence and love for God.

*"And without controversy great is the mystery of godliness: God was manifest in the flesh, justified in the Spirit, seen of angels, preached unto the nations, believed on in the world, received up into glory." (I Tim. 3:16).*

The reason this mystery is so defined is learned from the context in which it resides. The preceding context (vs. 14-15) has to do with the believer or the church's conduct while in the house of God as a testimony to the watching world without. The following context (4:1-3) reveals the godlessness that follows the departure from the faith. When people turn their backs on the path of faith, that is, when they abandon what they know intellectually to be true they become apostates. An apostate is one who deserts his faith (beliefs) and his principles. They may relate various reasons for taking this step but it always leads away from God's word and into a morass of godlessness. This is precisely the way many cults and sects have their beginning.

It must be noticed that a fruitful witness could not be made apart from Godliness. The Old Testament saints came to know this but they were never able to see Godliness portrayed in all its perfection. The only true demonstration of Godliness is to be seen in God's own Son incarnate. We are looking at one of the major reasons for the incarnation of Christ: God wanted to expose to all creation His perfect example of Godliness. He succeeded in doing this in the face of the most adverse of circumstances. The attributes of God could only be seen and appreciated as they became manifest in the life and work of the Son while walking among a fallen race of men. The text verse gives six features of Christ's incarnate ministry. These six scripturally inspired features are each a divinely distinguished subdivision of the entire gamut of the incarnate manifestation.

1) "God was manifest in the flesh." Jesus Christ was truly God in the likeness of man. His presence was the actual presence of God among men and could be seen and heard and felt. Jesus, like every man, was born of a woman; He came as a baby and grew and matured into a grown man. He had a body like all other men, consisting of flesh, blood, and bones. He was subject to physical infirmities in like pattern to His brethren – infirmities such as weariness, fatigue, hunger, thirst, and sleepiness. In this body of a man lived and dwelt the Eternal God, the Creator of all the universe. When He spoke, it was God speaking and when His action resulted in the miraculous, it was God working. "Then answered Jesus, and said unto them, Verily, verily, I say unto you, The Son can do nothing of himself, but what he seeth the Father do; for whatever things he doeth, these also doeth the Son in the same manner." (Jn. 5:19). The Scripture rightly says that one of His names is Emmanuel which means "God with us." It is to be regretted that this name, Emmanuel, is not better known or more widely used in Christian discussion or communication.

2) "Justified in the Spirit" Everything that Jesus did from birth to death (and beyond) was done in the Spirit. He was born of the Spirit (Lk. 1:35), He was filled of the Spirit, He was led by the Spirit (Lk. 4:1), His work was wrought by the Spirit (Lk. 4:18), Even in His death, His offering of Himself as a sacrifice for sin was done through the ministration of the Spirit. (Heb. 9:14) Everything that Jesus did and thought was right and good, and holy. During His trial His enemies had to resort to producing perjurers to falsely testify against Him. (Mk. 14:55-59). He was able to ask "which of you convinceth (convicteth) me of sin? And no man could step forward and answer the question with truth. His was a sinless, spotless life; if it were not so He could not be the Redeemer and Savior that He is. If justification truly is being declared righteous then being justified is a fit approbation for Jesus for

everything He did and said was in the perfection of the eternal Spirit. The New Testament affirms that "to him the Spirit was given without measure." (Jn. 3:34).

3) "Seen of angels" The angels have long been observers of their Creator and have shown intense interest in His activities carried out during His human experience right from their very beginning. It was an angel who announced His coming conception and resultant birth. (Lk. 1:26-38). Angels were present at the debut of His earthly life as a man. (Lk. 2:8-15). They were present at His resurrection, (Lk. 24:4) and again when He finished His visitation here on earth and ascended back to the heavenly realm into the presence of His Father (Acts 1:10-11). Even today the angels are still observing the effects of Jesus' work here on earth as they see men "born again" and the church being formed from believers from every nation on earth. The angels are interested observers of God's plan for men on earth, for through it they comprehend the many facets of God's manifold character. They had no other way to discern God's attributes except as those traits were exhibited in the plan of salvation for men. The angels knew God was holy but what is holiness apart from seeing it in comparison with sin and iniquity. They knew God was love but how can love be fully known without seeing it in its grandest hour - - at Calvary? The principal showcase of love in all the events of eternity was the hour when God gave His Son, His only Son, as the price for fallen man's redemption. "God so loved that He gave" (Jn. 3:16). The best description of love is giving. Through it all the angels, too, are learning of the wonderful, multifaceted wisdom of God. (Eph. 3:10).

4) "Preached unto Gentiles" It was never God's intent that He should be confined to be the God of one small nation of people. It is true that God spoke of Israel as "the apple of His eye" and that He loves that tiny nation "with an everlasting love." In the overall comprehensive plan of God, He has proven Himself to be the God of all mankind. The Bible says that "God so loved the world" (Jn. 3:16). God has moved from the narrow confines of serving one small elect nation to a much broader scope of redemption that reaches out to the whole human race. One of the last assurances God gives to men, all men, is an invitation when He says "Come --- whoever wishes, let him take the free gift of the water

of life." (Rev. 22:17). This can readily be seen as the literal fulfillment of God's promise to Abraham in Genesis 12:1-3 when God said, "In thee shall all families of the earth be blessed."

5) "Believed on in the world" Jesus said, "Go ye into all the world and preach the gospel to every creature" (Mk. 16:15). This portrays a vast turnaround from the experience of the Jews under "The Law" in the Old Testament. In those past days the law, the covenants, and the promises were all Jewish prerogatives and the Gentiles were almost exclusively without God and without hope. Now, by God's grace, in this the church age, the gospel of salvation is going out to all men and "whosoever will" may believe and be saved. Jesus had promised, "I will build my church" (Matt. 16:18) and this work has been progressing generation by generation down through the mystery age. Throughout the age there has been an unnumbered host taken from every kindred, tribe, and nation who have believed to the saving of their souls. (Rev. 5:9). The Bible says that the wall that once stood between the Jew and Gentile is now broken down and removed and of the two peoples God is making one new entity: The Church. (Eph. 2:14-15).

6) "Received up into glory", Some of the last words Jesus uttered before dying on the cross were "it is finished" and we now know He was referring to the work He came to do on earth. He once said "I came - - to do the will (work) of Him that sent me," (Jn. 6:38) and again He said "I have finished the work which thou gavest me to do." (Jn. 17:4) His return to the side of His Father in glory was a triumphal entrance, accompanied with joy, glory, and thanksgiving. This event was a victory celebration. He had closed this first phase of His work as absolute victor in all He came to achieve. His had been a most difficult and unpleasant task but He was successful in all that He undertook to do. Now the second phase of His work would begin; this is the ministry in which He has been engaged since His return to the Father in glory. His present ongoing ministry as the High Priest for the Church has a strong, firm foundation on which to repose. It was His successful work on earth that makes effective His meditorial ministry in the believer's behalf today.

## Chapter 9

Giants of the faith in the past were able to show to the world glimpses of what a life of Godliness could and would be like. Even in the lives of the Godliest of men this could only be a glimmer of a view, for all men are prone to error because each is burdened with a fallen sinful nature. It was not until the God-man, Jesus, came on the world scene that a complete picture of Godliness could be fully seen and appreciated. In our day men are without excuse; they have been given the perfect example of what God expects of every man. This measure of Godliness is attainable by all.

## Chapter X
## *THE MYSTERY OF INIQUITY*

*"For the mystery of iniquity doth already work; only he who now hindereth will continue to hinder until he be taken out of the way." (II Thess. 2:7).*

Man's will opposed to God's will as it is revealed in His Word is no mystery. But all lawlessness or self-will moving in a common direction toward the goal of being headed up in one powerful person posing as God is the mystery. The world today is passing through some of the darkest chapters in its history. Every phase of man's existence is being sorely tried in some form of crisis or another. The world is facing growing problems that are mushrooming faster than either men or their governments are able to cope.

God is a moral God, and the creation He brought into being and set in motion is most efficient when operating on moral principles. Governments of past generations and their citizens were in a general sense moral, but in just one generation, the pendulum has swung from a moral position through an amoral state and is now at best bordering on the immoral. Immorality has always been a curse of humanity in the form of greed, and selfishness, and the lust for power; but never in the pervasiveness prevalent in our time.

In the past several decades there has been a growing demand for personal or individual "rights". This demand is tearing down the whole social system that has been an institution for centuries. The Bible teaches the family -- husband, wife, and children -- is the social nucleus around which all else exists. It is this family social system that is under direct attack in this world's society of today. Columnist John Leo writing in the U.S. News and World Report of 11/30/92 in an article "On Society" said, "No society that hopes to survive can long tolerate family damage on this scale."

Things will continue to grow worse until men everywhere, in near desperation, will reach out to one seemingly super individual who shows promise to have answers to correct all the world's woes. This one man will be accepted by all the world as a savior - one who will be expected to bring peace and prosperity in a time those things are desperately needed. Time will reveal that this man's promises are hollow and full of lies and the world will come to know him as God has named him: the Antichrist.

The larger context from which the text of the mystery of iniquity has been extracted is as follows:

> *"Now we beseech you, brethren, by the coming of our Lord Jesus Christ, and by our gathering together unto him, that ye be not soon shaken in mind, or be troubled, neither by spirit, nor by word, nor by letter as from us, as that the day of Christ is at hand. Let no man deceive you by any means: for that day shall not come, except there be a falling away first, and that man of sin be revealed, the son of perdition; who opposeth and exalteth himself above all that is called God, or that is worshiped; so that he as God sitteth in the temple of God, shewing himself that he is God. Remember ye not, that, when I was yet with you, I told you these things? And now ye know what restraineth that he might be revealed in his time. For the <u>MYSTERY OF INIQUITY</u> doth already work: only he who now letteth will let, until he be taken out of the way. And then shall that wicked [one] be revealed, whom the Lord shall consume with the spirit of his mouth, and shall destroy with the brightness of his coming: even him, whose coming is after the working of Satan with all power and signs and lying wonders, and with all deceivableness of unrighteousness in them that perish; because they received not the love of the truth, that they might be saved."*
> *(II Thess. 2:1-10).*

In the sixth verse of this rather long quotation, an impersonal pronoun is used concerning the force that is restraining evil in the world today, and that restraining influence is no less than "the Church". Paul said "And now you know <u>WHAT</u> restraineth". In the seventh verse, the impersonal "WHAT" is changed to the personal "HE" as the Holy Spirit is given recognition for His ministry in the world today. After all, it is the presence of the Spirit within the Church that is the real restraining force being revealed here. The seventh verse says He "will continue to hinder (restrain) until He be taken out of the way." It is important to recognize that it is the rapture being spoken of, for the Spirit cannot depart without the Church departing also. The Lord Himself gave the strongest assurance of this fact at the time He gave the promise of the coming of the Spirit, for He said,

*"I will pray the Father, and he shall give you another Comforter, that he may abide with you FOREVER; even the Spirit of truth, whom the world cannot receive, because it seeth him not, neither knoweth him: but ye know him; for he dwelleth with you, and SHALL be <u>in</u> you. I will not leave you comfortless --." (Jn. 14:16-18).*

When the Holy Spirit is "taken out of the way" and the Church, of necessity, is taken with Him, there will be no longer any restraint upon the forces of evil. (II Thess. 2:8) says, "and THEN shall that wicked (one) be revealed." There is no reason to believe there is any time lag between the two verses or between the two events they portray. The "man of sin", antichrist, will come immediately upon the scene, and the tribulation period will blossom and flourish in all its horror. This is the man who demonically engineers the program for the extermination of Israel that ends in the battle of Armageddon and the "Second Coming" of Jesus "the Christ". This is a very graphic picture that God has described regarding the closing events of this age.

It is no accident that the "mystery of iniquity" appears where it does in the writings of the Apostle Paul. The two books to the church in Thessalonika frame the setting for this interesting study. The first book comforts saints about those who die in Christ before the rapture; that is, before the catching away of the church to be with the Lord. There were those who thought that the dead would miss out on the rapture and Paul writes to show this to be in error. The rapture is to include the whole church and not just the living saints. In order for this to be fully realized a resurrection of all the church saints of past ages would be necessitated and this is just what God has planned.

The second book to the Thessalonians is also written to bring comfort to the saints: only this time is to bring them assurance of the impossibility of the great tribulation overtaking them before the rapture occurs. The rapture will occur on what the Bible calls "the day of Christ", a great day for the Church. It is only after the Church is resurrected and raptured that the "day of the Lord" can come upon the world. The day of the Lord is an extended period of time, not just a single twenty four hour day, and it is a time of terrible wrath, judgment, and destruction.

*"Alas for the day! For the day of the LORD is at hand, and as a destruction from the Almighty shall it come." (Joel 1:15).*

*"Blow the trumpet in Zion, and sound an alarm in my holy mountain. Let all the inhabitants of the land tremble; for the day of the LORD cometh, for it is near at hand; a day of darkness and gloominess, a day of clouds and thick darkness, like the morning spread upon the mountains; a great people and a strong; there has not been ever the like, neither shall be any more after it, even to the years of many generations." (Joel 2:1-2).*

*"Woe unto you that desire the day of the LORD! To what end is it for you? The day of the LORD is darkness, and not light, as if a man did flee from a lion, and a bear met him; or went into the house, and leaned his hand on the wall, and a serpent bit him." (Amos 5:18-19).*

Many of the early first century saints suffered great persecution, even unto death. The spirit of antichrist was active in their day, the same spirit that put Jesus "the Christ" on the cross. Some thought they were already in the "great tribulation" and that the rapture had occurred and they had been left behind. Paul wrote to refute that error but also to show that in the last days error would wax worse and worse. The evil days will crescendo and culminate with antichrist having world wide dominion. The man of sin who is imbued with the spirit of antichrist, becomes the world leader and when at the zenith of his power will be a man indwelt by Satan himself. This man will be a dictator, a world ruler who is but a tool in the hands of a far more evil personality than that of his own contriving. Satan has said in the past "I will be like the Most High (Isa. 12:14) and quoting again he said to Adam "you will be as God" (Gen. 3:5). Now, putting these two diabolical ideas together, Satan thrusts his master plan on the gullible world. A Satan-controlled man in the place of God -- could there ever be a better formula for disaster? Yet that is exactly the program Satan is attempting to manipulate into being.

The world both past and present has observed many episodes of demon possession. The New Testament records a number of occasions when Jesus stepped in and, using His divine authority, ordered demons to leave certain individuals. Demon possession is only a prelude to the more serious revelation of the mystery of iniquity where Satan, the chief architect of the rebellion against God, becomes one of the main characters in the scene. Satan possession is of far graver consequence than the former condition of demon possession. A like plight is recorded of Judas (Lk. 22:3) as he prepared to betray Jesus to the Jewish religious leaders of his day. Satan lost the battle at Calvary when Jesus won the victory over sin and death; even so he will lose the battle here also when the man of sin shall be destroyed by the brightness of the glory at the Lord's presence. This is the program the mystery of iniquity is all about.

## Chapter XI
# THE MYSTERY OF THE CHURCH

*"For this cause I, Paul, the prisoner of Jesus Christ for you Gentiles—If ye have heard of the dispensation of the grace of God which is given me toward you, how that by revelation he made known unto me the <u>mystery</u> (as I wrote before in few words, By which, when ye read, ye may understand my knowledge in the <u>mystery of Christ</u>) Which in other ages was not made known unto the sons of men, as it is now revealed unto his holy apostles and prophets by the Spirit: That the Gentiles should be fellow heirs, and of the same body, and partakers of his promise in Christ by the gospel, Of which I was made a minister, according to the gift of the grace of God given unto me by the effectual working of his power. Unto me, who am less than the least of all saints, is this grace given, that I should preach among the Gentiles the unsearchable riches of Christ, And to make all men see what is the fellowship of the mystery, which from the beginning of the ages hath been hidden in God, who created all things by Jesus Christ, To the intent that now, unto the principalities and powers in heavenly places, might be known by the church the manifold wisdom of God, According to the eternal purpose which he purposed in Christ Jesus, our Lord, In whom we have boldness and access with confidence by the faith of him."*
(Eph. 3:1-12).

The Apostle Paul is the authority who speaks clearly on the subject of New Testament Mysteries, and especially is this true in his letter to the Ephesian church. Paul expends special effort to identify and describe the Church, the new entity that God is building and indwelling, in the new dispensation that has dawned upon the world. He refers to the church as the "mystery of Christ" which can be seen as appropriate, for the church and Christ can never be separated. The fact that the Scriptures name Christ the Head of the Church, which is His body, makes this statement all but undeniable. Paul points out that a special dispensation, or stewardship of the grace of God has been given to him in regards to this "mystery." Paul is the lone source of authority on this subject because he received the revelation from God with the stipulation that he would pass it on to others. Any today who would ignore the writings of the Apostle Paul, do so at their own peril, for Paul was the chosen instrument of God to disseminate this truth.

During the dispensation of law, God's intent and purpose was for Israel to be the witness to His power, glory, and salvation. Israel was to be the light in a lost and spiritually dark world, but the Jews, like any other self-righteous people, began to think of themselves and their knowledge of God as being superior and all others as pagan outsiders. Over the centuries this feeling of superiority slowly but surely built a wall around the Jews and separated them from the rest of the nations of the world. It is true that God wanted them to be a different people, a holy people, a nation that reflected His glory. But it was a radically different kind of separation that developed. Israel substituted a facade of ritual service for the real walk with God, and in doing so they lost their witness, they lost their uniqueness, and they lost their blessing. This wall of separation between the Jews and the rest of mankind was artificial at best, and basically was constructed on a foundation of hypocrisy. The Jews estimation of themselves, their holiness, their righteousness, etc. was far higher than their appearance in the eyes of their Creator.

The wall that separated the Jews from their Gentile neighbors was one of pride and superiority in their own minds. It took a more tangible form after the temple was built. The temple was supposed to be the House of God, and it was there the Shekinah Glory resided for centuries. It was there also that the Ark of the Covenant was located in the most holy place, behind the veil. God had told this people,

# Chapter 11

> *"And there will I meet with thee, and I will commune with thee from above the mercy seat, from between the two cherubim which are upon the ark of testimony, -- ."* (Ex. 25:22).

This is where the people came to worship God. In the courtyard that had to be crossed to gain entrance to the temple proper, was a low dividing wall. The area between the entrance gate and this wall was called the court of the Gentiles. Any non-Jew could freely enter this court but was forbidden to pass beyond the parting wall. To do so would be to court almost certain death. The Gentile was not allowed to get close to God.

One day, some years ago, I was talking to a Jew and he repeated a little anecdote that I thought was very interesting and pertinent to this subject. I cannot vouch for the veracity of his facts, but still they are fascinating. He said that the low parting wall of which we are speaking, had a name. It was called "the fanum" and when a non-Jew came up to that wall and stood there before it, he was referred to as being profanum. This is the origin of the English word "profane" of which the dictionary says it means "outside the temple, hence, unsacred." When the Bible speaks in Ephesians chapter two of breaking down the middle wall of partition that stood between the Jew and the Gentile, it is probably speaking of the immaterial wall built in men's minds. But with the destruction of the Jewish temple in the year 70 AD, the more material wall was removed also. Today, both Jew and Gentile have equal right and ability to approach God and be saved. Through the power of the Holy Spirit in the act of regeneration, both become Christian and members of the Body of Christ, The Church.

It was God's desire that the nation Israel would demonstrate His presence by living godly and righteously, and thereby become an example to the Gentile nations. These nations, after witnessing God's blessing on Israel would then emulate this example in an attempt to walk the same path with the end result being a race of men exercising godliness and living in a period of great peace. It has always been the determination of God to show Himself as the God of all men and not just the God of Israel.

The wall of separation that developed was produced by Israel's action and was not of God's doing, but God, having foreseen the waywardness of the human heart and knowing the direction Israel would choose, had devised a far superior plan to put into execution in the affairs of men at this time. The "mystery of the church" reveals how God's purpose was to destroy the wall of separation and incorporate both believing Jews and Gentiles into one new body. The Apostle Paul was one of the first to see the direction of this new divine purpose, and he put it into words when he wrote,

*"For there is no difference between the Jew and the Greek; (Gentile) for the same Lord over all is rich unto all that call upon him." (Ro. 10:12).*

In breaking down the middle wall of partition, God instituted a new project, a New Testament mystery totally without Old Testament revelation, intentionally unrevealed. This mystery came upon the world with startling suddenness and virtually no fanfare. It should be observed that one of the leading features of this "mystery" is not merely that the regenerated Jew and Gentile are brought into joint blessing, but that "in Christ" they are no longer Jew and Gentile. Both are of one new living spiritual organism, the body of which Christ is the head.

*"For He Himself is our peace, who hath made both groups into one, and broke down the barrier of the dividing wall, by abolishing in His flesh the enmity, which is the Law of commandments contained in ordinances, that in Himself He might make the two into one new man, thus establishing peace." (Eph. 2:14-15). NASB*

The church age, commonly called the age of grace, is an interruption in the age of law; actually occurring within the parameters of the later age. The age of law began with Israel camped at Mt. Sinai (Ex. 19) and it will end at the second Advent of the Lord when He comes to install the Messianic Kingdom. (Rev. 19:11). The entire church age also runs its course between those two events, although as history shows, the church had its beginning many centuries after Moses trod on Mt. Sinai. The age of law was in force for fifteen hundred years before the Church began and it will again be in force for some period of time after the Church is "caught up" and no longer on earth. James, who presided over what was probably the first ever church council, said,

> *"Men and brethren, hearken unto me: Simon hath declared how God first did visit the nations, to take out of them a people for his name. And to this agree the words of the prophets, as it is written: After this I will return, and will build again the tabernacle of David, which is fallen down; and I will build again its ruins, and I will set it up; That the residue of men might seek after the Lord, and all the nations, upon whom my name is called, saith the Lord, who doeth all these things." (Acts 15:13-17).*

The Church is the supreme purpose of God in the present age. It consists of those people, called out of the world, who are in spiritual union with Christ, and acknowledge Him as their head. They are indwelt by the Spirit and made members of one another as they glorify God the Father. It is the indissoluble union with Christ that is the great distinction of the Church. This relationship is so complex that the New Testament uses no less than seven different illustrations to carry the point, each illustration adding one or more salient facts. The seven are:

| | |
|---|---|
| 1) The Shepherd and the Sheep | John 10:1-16 |
| 2) The Vine and the Branches | John 15:1-5 |
| 3) The Head and Members | Eph. 1:22-23 |
| 4) The Cornerstone and Living Stones | Eph. 2:20-22 |
| 5) The Last Adam and the New Creation | Eph. 3:1-12 |
| 6) The Bridegroom and the Bride | Eph. 5:22-23 |
| 7) The High Priest and the Kingdom of Priests | Heb. 7:12-22 |

## *The Shepherd and the Sheep*

*"I am the good shepherd; the good shepherd giveth his life for the sheep." (Jn. 10:11).*

*"I am the good shepherd, and know my sheep, and am known of mine. As the Father knoweth me, even so know I the Father; and I lay down my life for the sheep. And other sheep I have, that are not of this fold; them also I must bring, and they shall hear my voice; and there shall be one fold and one shepherd. Therefore doth my Father love me, because I lay down my life, that I might take it again." (Jn. 10:14-17).*

The people of Israel were the "sheep of his pasture" (Psa. 100:3), but in John chapter ten the sheep are not being led into the fold, but rather they are led out of it. Psalm twenty-three says the sheep lie down in green pastures and are led by still waters. Those expressions indicate activity outside the fold. The inference being that Jewish believers are led out of Judaism (Israel's fold) and together with other sheep, Gentile believers, will form one flock. Judaism was a fold but the fold no longer exists; there is only one flock and one Shepherd.

Jesus said "I am come that they might have life" (Jn. 10:10), and this was accomplished by Him as the Good Shepherd, laying down His own life for His sheep and proving His love at great cost to Himself. The hireling is not personally concerned with the sheep, whereas between the Good Shepherd and His own flock exists a bond of tender intimacy. This bond of intimacy amounts to a communion of understanding, and it is a communion that flows in both directions, from Shepherd to sheep and back to the Shepherd. The Scriptures emphasize the point that the sheep know the voice of the Shepherd.

*" -- the sheep hear his voice; and he calleth his own sheep by name, and leadeth them out. And when he putteth forth his own sheep, he goeth before them, and the sheep follow him; for they know his voice. And a stranger will they not follow, but will flee from him; for they know not the voice of strangers." (Jn. 10:3-5).*

What a truly wonderful statement; the sheep know His voice. Our Father has prepared a salvation for us, His children, to which nothing could be added that would make an appreciable improvement upon it. He has given us the gift of the Holy Spirit. One of the first things said concerning this gift is He would teach us the Word. The Word is the voice of God.

*"But the Comforter, who is the Holy Spirit, whom the Father will send in my name, he shall <u>teach</u> you all things, and bring all things to your remembrance, whatever I have said unto you." (Jn. 14:26).*

Every believer should be absorbed by the Word, and then let the Word saturate him or her through and through. When this becomes an actuality a number of other things begin to happen just as He promised.

*"If any man will do his will, he shall know of the doctrine, whether it be of God," (Jn. 7:17).*

It is the Spirit working within that is the key to so much of the blessing the Father is both willing and waiting to pour out on us. It was the Apostle Paul who said "The Spirit Himself beareth witness with our spirit, that we are the children of God." (Ro. 8:16). Daily use of the Scriptures will produce surprising results, and with frequent reading and review it almost becomes automatic to begin to memorize special verses or portions. With the ever present aid of the Holy Spirit, the precepts of God almost become second nature and decisions can be made without a lot of agonizing.

*"For everyone that useth milk is unskillful in the word of righteousness; for he is a babe. But solid food belongeth to them that are of full age, even those who by reason of use have their senses exercised to discern both good and evil." (Heb. 5:13-14).*

The Good Shepherd said "I <u>know</u> my sheep, and am <u>known</u> of mine" (Jn. 10:14) This intimate relationship that exists between Shepherd and sheep is but a reflection of the relationship between the Savior and the saved (believers). The Shepherd not only knows the names of His individual sheep, but He faithfully records each name in the book of life. This activity on the part of the Shepherd is very important to the sheep for their security as well as their peace of mind. At the time of the final judgment, this same book of life will be opened and used as a last check as a guarantee of the sheeps' safety.

> " -- and the books were opened; and another book was opened, which is the book of life. -- And whosoever was not found written in the book of life was cast into the lake of fire." (Rev. 20:12, 15).

As the <u>Good</u> Shepherd He gave His life for the sheep; but even as He did so He said, "I lay down My life, that I might take it again." (Jn. 10:17) It was never Jesus' intent to leave the sheep without a leader, and the New Testament goes on to enlarge the emerging picture of the Shepherd as it reveals Jesus as the <u>Great</u> Shepherd. "Now the God of peace, that brought again from the dead our Lord Jesus, that great Shepherd of the sheep,— " (Heb. 13:20). The Great Shepherd is the resurrected Lord, never to die again, always ready to care for His own. He leads, feeds, and intercedes for His sheep whom the Father has given to Him. (Jn. 17:9, 11-12). The picture is completed and His role as that of the <u>Chief</u> Shepherd is revealed by the Apostle Peter, as he tells how Jesus will be coming again to the earth.

> "And when the <u>chief</u> Shepherd shall appear, ye shall receive a crown of glory that fadeth not away." (I Pet. 5:4)

The outstanding features to be noted in this illustration of the Shepherd and the sheep are: 1) the sheep are to expect leadership, protection, and sustenance from the Shepherd while in turn; 2) the Shepherd can expect obedience and tractability from His flock. There is a complete relationship established between Shepherd and flock that will endure throughout the ages.

## *The Vine and the Branches*

> "I am the true vine, and my Father is the vinedresser. Every branch in me that beareth not fruit he taketh away; and every

*branch that beareth fruit, he purgeth it, that it may bring forth more fruit. Now ye are clean through the word which I have spoken unto you. Abide in me, and I in you. As the branch cannot bear fruit of itself, except it abide in the vine, no more can ye, except ye abide in me. I am the vine, ye are the branches. He that abideth in me, and I in him, the same bringeth forth much fruit; for without me ye can do nothing." (Jn. 15:1-5).*

The foremost element in the illustration of the Vine and Branches is that of fruit bearing. The one sure requirement of fruit bearing is the branch "abiding" in the vine. For the illustration to maintain maximum effectiveness, the "union" of vine and branch must be assumed, for one of the first things said, in verse two, is "every branch in me."

The narrative of the Vine and the Branches is not propounding the idea that a believer is lost if he is not fruitful. Again, the opening statement designates a branch "in him" that does not bear fruit. The Lord desires all believers to be fruitful and the illustration reveals even that branch which bears fruit will be purged and pruned with the intent that it bear yet more fruit. The branch that continues to bear no fruit at all is said to be "taken away", which could well mean premature departure from this life, snatched up into heaven itself. This would parallel the teaching of the Apostle Paul in First Corinthians where he speaks of believers dying for their failure to walk pleasing to the Lord, physical death not being equated with condemnation.

*"But let a man examine himself, and so let him eat of that bread, and drink of that cup. For he that eateth and drinketh unworthily, eateth and drinketh judgment to himself, not discerning the Lord's body. For this cause many are weak and sickly among you, and many sleep (die)." (I Cor. 11:28-30).*

Premature death carries its own penalties such as loss of rewards for good deeds not done, loss of treasure to be stored up in heaven, loss of blessing here on earth: loss, loss, loss.

Fruitfulness depends on one's abiding in Christ and is one of the most important factors in God's plan for men in this present age. Fruit is the product of the vine whose life giving vitality is imparted to the branches. Of the major factors to be seen in the illustration of the Vine, the most important is that a common life is exhibited throughout all—the root, the vine, and the branches; but it is only in the branches that fruit is to be found.

Abiding in Christ or in His Word results in ongoing, day by day communion with God. In contrast, union with Christ only comes about by an act of God, and is irreversible; it is a one time only occurrence. Fruitfulness is dependent on abiding in Christ, something that every believer is instructed to strive to obtain. Abiding, with its corresponding communion, requires human effort: obedience, discipline, will—all are brought into participation. Abiding in Christ indicates unbroken communion with God on the part of the one who has entered unalterable union with Christ.

## *The Head and Members*

*"And hath put all things under his feet, and gave him to be the head over all things to the church, Which is his body, the fullness of him that filleth all in all." (Eph. 1:22-23).*

*"For as the body is one, and hath many members, and all the members of that body, being many, are one body, so also is Christ. For by one Spirit were we all baptized into one body, whether we be Jews or Greeks, whether we be bond or free; and have been all made to drink into one Spirit. For the body is not one member, but many. (I Cor. 12:12-14).*

*"But now hath God set the members, every one of them, in the body, as it hath pleased him. --- But now are they many members, yet one body. --- Now ye are the body of Christ, and members in particular." (I Cor. 12:18, 20, 27).*

The figure of the human body is the most frequently used illustration to represent the relationship between Christ and the Church. Because every individual has a body, they can easily identify and understand the activities of the various members of the body as they function in accordance to the will of the head. The true Church is an organism, which indicates it has a common life, the Holy Spirit, throughout all its members. The life that energizes the head with its eyes, ears, and mouth is the same life that activates the arms, legs, and toes. As it was in the story of the Vine and Branches, a vital union to Christ is the central truth which this new figure sets forth. No other people past or future will ever occupy the blessed and distinct position The Church has as the Body of Christ. There is a relationship here, a kinship, ordained of God, beautiful in its conception and composition and reserved for believers of this age only. Because this is revealed as a New Testament mystery, no such relationship as described herein was ever obtained in the Old Testament order, nor will it apply in the future kingdom age.

In the true Church, the mystic body of which Christ is the head, every member has been baptized into the one body and been made to drink into one Spirit. (I Cor. 12:13). The members come from an extremely varied background; the Jews from a seemingly advantages position, the Gentiles being looked upon as rank outsiders. Nevertheless, the Bible says there is no difference: these widely divergent persons are all of the same standing - sinners - and all as believers become members of the same body through regeneration by an act of the Spirit. Since there is one life common to all members, there should be smooth, unabrasive cooperation between members to avoid any possible irritation. It is very apparent to most observers that there is great failure on this very point in much of christendom in our time. As christendom is brought into view, it is important to remember that the True Church and christendom are not identical; these words are not synonyms. Christendom is much wider and more encompassing in its coverage than the Church, the mystical body of Christ. Christendom is synonymous with the Kingdom of Heaven during the mystery age. (See chapter I ). To everyone's shame almost continual strife is carried on between the different segments of the visible church on earth. This is understandable knowing that the visible church contains both wheat and tares, believers mingled with unbelievers. One can see the same blight at work in the True Church, but in this case it is mainly the result of ignorance of God's word, either not knowing the word or misinterpreting what they read.

It is this figure of the head and body that so remarkably indicates a number of essential realities respecting the Church that are being brought to the attention, namely: 1) the Church is a continually self-developing body, 2) each of its members is designed for a specific service, and, 3) In all its diversity, it retains its unity, it is <u>one body</u>.

1) The Church as a Self-Developing Body. The Lord Jesus Himself left a prophetic promise with His disciples that would have great influence on the yet-to-be Church. He said "And I say also unto thee, that thou art Peter, and upon this rock I will build my church, and the gates of Hades shall not prevail against it." (Matt. 16:18). Hades is the Greek word for "the place of departed souls." The Greek word Hades is the equivalent of the Hebrew word sheol and is understood to be the temporary abode of the dead, all the dead; it is the realm of all departed souls. As the body goes into the grave, the soul goes into Hades. The Lord Himself was no exception to this rule. His body was placed in a borrowed tomb but He is seen going about His business completing the work He came to do. The Apostles tell us,

> *"For Christ also hath once suffered for sins, the just for the unjust, that he might bring us to God, being put to death in the flesh but made alive by the Spirit, by which also he went and preached unto the <u>spirits in prison</u>, who once were disobedient, -- ." (I Pet. 3:18-20).*

The Lord spent a comparatively short time in Hades, just three days. In that brief time it is said, He preached to the captives. Hades is shown to be a divided place with two distinct compartments separated from each other by a great fixed gulf. (Lk. 16:26). The saved dead of all the past generations are in one section which is called "paradise," (Lk. 23:43) or Abraham's bosom, (Lk. 16:22-23) and the unsaved or ungodly are in the second section which retains the name Hades. In the past, the two groups were within sight and speaking distance of each other but because of the gulf between they could not intermingle. The Lord spent three days preaching to these individuals and persuading them that the events taking place at that time were the fulfillment of all the ceremonial and sacrificial types that were demanded of them in the past. In effect the Lord was saying, "This is what it was all about".

## Chapter 11

After His three day stay in Hades He was resurrected from among the dead and the Bible says that "when he ascended up on high, he led captivity captive, --." (Eph. 4:8). Today, Hades is an even more widely divided realm than previously seen, with that part occupied by the saved dead now being in the presence of the Lord in heaven. The Scriptures say,

*"Therefore, we are always confident, knowing that, while we are at home in the body, we are absent from the Lord (For we walk by faith, not by sight); we are confident, I say, and willing rather to be absent from the body, and to be present with the Lord. Wherefore, we labor that, whether present or absent, we may be accepted of him." (II Cor. 5:6-9).*

The Lord has stated in the form of a promise that the Church would be a continuous, growing, renewing organism that would not cease to exist with the passing of any single generation of the saints. The passing of any one generation of believers would not jeopardize the life or even the health of a vigorous, vital, victorious Church in which the Spirit of God resided. The Apostle Paul, who had so much to do with the establishment and growth of the early church, was also the one who gave instruction on how this self-development ability of the Church was to work.

*"And he gave some, apostles; and some, prophets; and some, evangelists; and some, pastors and teachers; For the perfecting of the saints for the work of the ministry for the edifying of the body of Christ." (Eph. 4:11-12).*

The ministry of gifted men was for a particular service: to perfect the saints to fit them for their continued ministry among other saints in the growing Church. The obligation to use one's gift(s) and to be a witness of the resurrected Christ rests upon every Christian alike. Young believers need to be trained and God has given direction how this goal is to be accomplished. New believers are to be "equipped" for service by the gifted men He has placed over them as their leaders. Pastors and teachers must be properly trained for their leadership role in the local churches. Leaders in most other fields such as business and industry are required to have extensive education. The pastor/teacher has a much greater responsibility in that he is dealing with the soul's of men and with heavenly things. Today, the preparation of church leaders is largely left in the hands of professors in theological seminaries, and far too often these are the men failing in their God given responsibilities. From many seminaries it is a very uncertain sound that is being heard in the fields of doctrine, soul-winning, and missions. What wonderful changes would be seen, revival fires ignited, spiritual forces released, if the churches would demand the purification of the fountain sources of their doctrinal teaching.

The individual member does not choose his place in the body but this disposition is reserved by God for the exclusive exercise of His sovereign will. It is God's inalienable right to establish both the position and the consequent duties of each believer. The Bible says "But now hath God set the members, every one of them, in the body, as it hath pleased him." (I Cor. 12:18). This reference is re-enforced by the Word in Romans which recognizes this same sovereign purpose in respect to the specific activity of each and every member of the body. There it is written,

*"For I say, through the grace given unto me, to every man that is among you, not to think of himself more highly than he ought to think, but to think soberly, according as God hath dealt to every man the measure of faith." (Ro. 12:3).*

The different members have different purposes and God has equipped them with different gifts, thus there should be no grounds for petty jealousy or strife. All members are equally necessary and all will be equally rewarded for faithful service. Intelligent soul-winning service by the Church with all members operating efficiently is the New Testament standard.

## *The Cornerstone and Living Stones*

*"Now, therefore, ye are no more strangers and sojourners, but fellow citizens with the saints, and of the household of God;*

# Chapter 11

*And are built upon the foundation of the apostles and prophets, Jesus Christ himself being the chief corner stone, In whom all the building fitly framed together groweth unto an holy temple in the Lord; In whom ye also are built together for an habitation of God through the Spirit." (Eph. 2:19-22).*

The definition of a cornerstone as given in the Readers Digest Great Encyclopedic Dictionary is listed as follows:

1) *A stone uniting two walls at the corner of a building.*

2) *Such a stone, often inscribed, and made into a repository for documents, laid into the foundation of an edifice.*

3) *Something of primary importance.*

When used in describing Christ's relation to the Church all three of these definitions become very applicable. The use of a stone or a rock as an illustration of the Lord is quite common in the Old Testament and therefore does not fall into the category of belonging as part of a New Testament mystery. To Israel He is said to be the stone the builders rejected.

*"The stone which the builders refused is become the head of the corner. This is the Lord's doing; it is marvelous in our eyes." (Psa. 118:22-23).*

It was because He was rejected by Israel that He became a stumbling block to that nation.

*"And he shall be for a sanctuary; but for a stone of stumbling and for a rock of offense to both the houses of Israel, for a trap and for a snare to the inhabitants of Jerusalem. And many among them shall stumble, and fall, and be broken, and be snared, and be taken." (Isa. 8:14-15).*

In the prophetic picture, the Lord is shown to have a role as a stone also to the Gentile nations; for to them He is called the smiting stone.

> *"Thou sawest until a stone was cut out without hands, which smote the image upon its feet that were of iron and clay, and broke them to pieces."* (Dan. 2:34).

The image mentioned in this portion of Daniel's prophecy represents the course of Gentile world supremacy. The various parts of the image represented different kingdoms or empires, beginning with the head and ending at the feet which consisted of two different incompatible materials. The feet portray the final form of Gentile world government and it is here the stone, typifying Christ, strikes and destroys the whole structure. It is at His second coming, when Christ comes as LORD of lords and King of kings, having all power and all authority, that He puts an end to Gentile world supremacy and smashes all the world's governments. He then sets up His own ruling authority and the Messianic Kingdom dawns.

> *"Jesus saith unto them, Did ye never read in the scriptures, The stone which the builders rejected, the same is become the head of the corner; this is the Lord's doing, and it is marvelous in our eyes? Therefore say I unto you, The kingdom of God shall be taken from you, and given to a nation bringing forth the fruits of it. And whosoever shall fall on this stone shall be broken, but on whomsoever it shall fall, it will grind him to powder."* (Matt. 21:42-44).

In this passage can be seen all three of the types of Christ as a stone. 1) He becomes the destroyer of all Gentile authority, 2) He is the Stumbling Stone to Israel, and, 3) He is the Foundation Stone on which the Church is built. This is the prophetic pronouncement that should have awakened men to the fact that a transition period was imminent in which God's former divine purpose with Israel would give way to the now divine purpose for the Church. He forecasts the fall of Israel as they stumble over Him as the "rock of offence" and that one day, still future, the Gentiles would "be ground to powder" in judgment under that same Rock now referred to as the Smiting Stone.

Looking at the Church as it is being formed in this age, the figure of a stone remains as an apt designation of the Lord and His place in the fabrication of this edifice. He is seen as a highly proficient, irreplaceable, cornerstone, the key element of the whole structure. In this temple, which is the Church, Gentile believers are no longer "strangers and foreigners" (Eph. 2:19) but they are said to be "fellow citizens with the saints, and of the household of God." This is an infinitely higher calling than any proffered to the people of Israel under all their wonderful covenant privileges. Israel produced many saints in past ages, but without exception none ever experienced a relationship to, or knowledge of, the Church as it is being formed in this present age by the Spirit. Israel indeed had a temple in which they could meet and worship the Living God, but the Church is a temple, the residence of the Holy Spirit, the third person of the God Head.

To those who have worked in building construction, the place and use of a cornerstone is well known. It is something of primary importance. The cornerstone establishes the corner, usually a right angle, from which the length and width are marked off. In addition, all the elevations of the different levels are determined from this principal point and a plumb line to the cornerstone fixes the vertical accuracy of the edifice. Important indeed. The cornerstone sets the standards for the entire building. This is precisely what the Lord Jesus does as Chief Cornerstone for the Church.

The definition of a cornerstone included the fact that it often was a repository for documents and this is a most apt description of Christ in His ministry to men. He is the Living Word who came to reveal the Father to a lost and perishing race. The Bible says of Him,

> *"In the beginning was the Word, and the Word was with God, and the Word was God. --- And the Word was made flesh, and dwelt among us (and we beheld his glory, the glory as of the only begotten of the Father], full of grace and truth. --- No man hath seen God at any time; the only begotten Son, who is in the bosom of the Father, he hath declared him." (Jn. 1:1, 14, 18).*

In our time, God, through the Spirit, dwells in the Church which is the temple of God. This temple is not a building made by men, it is not a church building, it is not even a material structure. (Acts 7:47-50). God dwells in the hearts of those who have trusted in Christ; thus He indwells the individual believer and in the larger view He lives in the Church collectively.

> *"What? Know ye not your body is the temple of the Holy Spirit who is in you, whom ye have of God, and ye are not your own? For ye are bought with a price; therefore, glorify God in your body and in your spirit, which are God's." (I Cor. 6:19-20).*

The foundation for this Church was laid by the apostles and the New Testament prophets; the foundation being the Lord Jesus Himself, who is also the chief cornerstone.

> *"For other foundation can no man lay than that which is laid, which is Jesus Christ." (I Cor. 3:11).*

This temple is "fitly framed together" so that every part, each living stone, accomplishes the purpose that God intended for them. The Church is said to be the temple in which the Spirit of God resides during His present ministry among men. It consists of all the regenerated saints of this age, approximately 60 generations, allowing 33 years for each generation. Every Christian is likened to a living stone because each is indwelt by the Spirit of God and as such is designed and shaped by the Spirit to fit into a certain specific place in the overall structure. The Bible says, "But Christ as a son over his own house, whose house are we,— " (Heb. 3:6).

> *"Ye also, as living stones, are built up a spiritual house, an holy priesthood, to offer up spiritual sacrifices, acceptable to God by Jesus Christ. (I Pet. 2:5).*

The foundation for the Church was laid by the apostles and the New Testament prophets and this foundation is the Lord Himself, who also is declared to be the chief cornerstone. The Word says,

> *"The stone which the builders refused is become the head stone of the corner. This is the Lord's doing; it is marvelous in our eyes. This is the day that the Lord hath made; we will rejoice and be glad in it." (Psa. 118:22-24).*

Speaking of Christ's resurrection, the Apostle Peter tells how prophecy was fulfilled when he declared "this is the stone set at nought of you builders, which has become the head of the corner." (Acts 4:11). This temple, otherwise known as the Church, the dwelling place of God, is a building "fitly framed together" so that every part, each living stone, accomplishes the purpose that God has for them.

## *The Last Adam and a New Creation*

*"And so it is written, The first man, Adam, was made a living soul; the last Adam was made a life-giving spirit." (I Cor. 15:45).*

In the story of creation, the Bible tells of God creating the first man, Adam, who then became the head of the human race. More than that, Adam is discovered to be the federal head of the race. As used in this manner federal means representative, and Adam at creation was designated to represent all men who came after him. As Adam acted, the race acted. When Adam sinned and fell from fellowship with God, the whole race of men whom he represented also sinned and fell from fellowship. The Bible says "Wherefore, as by one man sin entered the world, and death by sin, and so death passed upon all men, for all sinned." (Ro. 5:12). This one act by the federal head left the entire race that came after Adam in a helpless, hopeless condition with no seeming way out. God was well aware of man's situation and many times the Scriptures speak of the Creator's love for the creature man. So to man's eternal good, when he could do nothing for himself, the Bible says BUT GOD — did something.

*"The Lord is not slack concerning his promise, as some men count slackness, but is long-suffering toward us, not willing that any should perish, but that all should come to repentance." (II Pet. 3:9).*

*"For God so loved the world, that he gave his only begotten Son, that whosoever believeth in him should not perish, but have everlasting life." (Jn. 3:16).*

At this point a series of strands of doctrine combine together, and as they do they form a strong cord upon which believers of the past twenty centuries have hung their hopes, their lives, and their future. The Bible says,

1) "The wages of sin is death." (Ro. 6:23).

2) Christ is the sinless Son of God in whom there was found no grounds for death.

3) Man's sin was imputed (charged) to Christ. (Ro. 4:25)

4) Christ took the sinners place as a substitute and "died for the ungodly." (Ro. 5:6,8)

5) He is the infinite Son of God and His infinite life was of greater value than the sum total of the lives of all finite men.

6) A Holy God was completely satisfied with the price paid for sin.

7) God's holiness having been satisfied, Jesus arose victorious over death.

8) The resurrected Jesus is the first of a new race of men; thus He is the representative head of this new race and is called the last Adam. (Ro. 6:8, 11).

9) Christ's righteousness is imputed to all believers; thus if He is acceptable to the Father, so are we who believe.

10) All men who experience regeneration are new creatures and are members of a new creation.

When Christ arose after His death and burial, He ushered in a whole new sphere of reality, a new creation that had not existed before. He was now clothed with an immortal, glorified body which has become the pattern to which all saints will attain, the fulfillment of the "blessed hope." (Titus 2:13). This New Creation is a direct result of union with

Christ and can be attributed to the work of the Holy Spirit. The New Testament tells plainly,

> *"Therefore, if any man be in Christ, he is a new creation; old things are passed away; behold, all things are become new. And all things are of God who hath reconciled us to himself by Jesus Christ ---." (II Cor. 5:17-18).*

> *"The first man is of the earth, earthy; the second man is the Lord from heaven. As is the earthy, such are they also that are earthy; and as is the heavenly, such are they also that are heavenly. And as we have borne the image of the earthy, we shall bear the image of the heavenly. (I Cor. 15:47-49).*

Without Christ none of this is possible. God has built this program around His Son, and apart from faith in the work that Christ carried out to completion, there is no hope, no salvation. The Scriptures give verification to this truth by saying "For in Christ Jesus neither circumcision availeth anything, nor uncircumcision, but a new creature." (Gal. 6:15). All the religious ceremonies man can devise, all the good works he may do, all avail nothing without Christ. A vital union with the Lord of Glory is the key to immeasurable value -- a new creation and eternal life.

The resurrection of Christ is unto a new creation. Christ's resurrection was not a mere reversal of the death process as it is usually and most naturally assumed. All other accounts in the Scriptures of so-called resurrections were but restorations to a former existence. These people were returned to a mortal estate, to a natural, physical condition from which they eventually died again. Not so with Christ; He was raised from among the dead as a different, an entirely new kind of being. He came forth in a body wonderfully transformed from the one in which He was humiliated, suffered and died. His was now a "glorious body;" a body consisting of flesh and bones but — with no blood. Eight days after His resurrection, He challenged His disciple, Thomas, to thrust his finger and his hand into the open wounds He still displayed. (Jn. 20:25). These wounds were not closed scars; they give sure proof of a bloodless body. God said of the natural man that the life was in the blood. (Gen. 9:4). In the resurrected Christ we see something the world had never encountered before. Here is life on an entirely different principle: a body, a true physical body, immortal, incorruptible, one suited for both heaven and eternity. Some believe and teach that Christ was resurrected as a spirit but spirits are never buried, only bodies. If language is to remain a reliable means of communication, then it must be granted that in a resurrection that which went into the grave, a body, is what comes out again.

Of the seven illustrations applied to the Church none is of more importance than this one declaring the new organism to be a New Creation. Not only is each member composing the Church a newly created being, but the entire company is related to Christ who is its Federal Head. This New Creation is incorporated along with Christ into one new identity: the Church. Christ, in his resurrected life, is the representative head of a new race of men, born again ones who are called the children of God. He is the Federal head of this new creation, and with this position He has the title of the last Adam.

> *"Behold, what manner of love the Father hath bestowed upon us, that we should be called the children of God; therefore, the world knoweth us not, because it knew him not. Beloved, now are we the children of God, and it doth not yet appear what we shall be, but we know that, when he shall appear, we shall be like him; for we shall see him as he is."* (I Jn. 3:1-2).

This new creation is rendered viable by the believer's direct organic union with Christ. There has been a complete removal, by way of death, of the former existence of the natural or Adamic man. This removal or termination came about through the substitutionary death of Christ in our place. This is judicial language but in the Bible it is written this way,

> *"How shall we that are dead (who died) to sin, live any longer therein? Know ye not, that so many of us as were baptized into Jesus Christ were baptized into his death? Therefore we are buried with him by baptism into death: that like as Christ was raised up from the dead by the glory of the Father, even so we also should walk in newness of life."* (Ro. 6:2-4).

Chapter 11

Christ died for the sin of the whole world. As our substitute our sin was imputed (charged) to Him and He died because of it. In a perfect act of substitution for those who are "in Christ", His resurrection is proof our sin is gone, and with His righteousness imputed (charged) to us, we are fully justified in God's sight. This great truth is best seen in the Word,

> *"If ye then be risen with Christ, seek those things which are above, where Christ sitteth on the right hand of God. Set your affection on things above, not on things on the earth. For ye are dead (ye died) and your life is hid with Christ in God. When Christ, who is our life, shall appear, then shall ye also appear with him in glory." (Col. 3:1-4).*

As the Bride and wife of the King of Kings, the Church is actually His consort and will share in His reign. In this position she is not a subject of the King, but she sits beside Him and assists in the governing rather than being governed. This wonderful truth is supported by the Word which says,

> *"Blessed and holy is he that hath part in the first resurrection; on such the second death hath no power, but they shall be priests of God and of Christ, and shall <u>reign</u> with him a thousand years." (Rev. 20:6).*

The Savior is called a King-priest, and the Church collectively is referred to as a "<u>royal</u> priesthood," for the Apostle Peter uses that term in his epistle. He wrote "But ye are a chosen generation, a royal priesthood, an holy nation, a people of his own, that ye should show forth the praises of him who called you out of darkness into his marvelous light." (I Pet. 2:9).

## *The Bridegroom and the Bride*

> *"For the husband is the head of the wife, even as Christ is the head of the church; --- Therefore, as the church is subject unto Christ, --- (for) Christ also loved the church, and gave himself for it, That he might sanctify and cleanse it with the washing of*

*water by the Word; That he might present it to himself a glorious church, not having spot, or wrinkle, or any such thing; but that it should be holy and without blemish." (Eph. 5:23-27).*

This illustration precipitates a view of a strong contrast between Israel and the Church. The Church in the New Testament is seen as the Virgin Bride: spotless and chaste. The text passage taken from Ephesians chapter five, gives a three fold view of the relationship that exists between the Church and the Lord.

| | | |
|---|---|---|
| past: | Christ gave Himself for it. (the Church) | vs. 25 |
| present: | that He might sanctify it. | vs. 26 |
| future: | that He might present it to Himself. | vs. 27 |

Israel is dismayingly pictured as the unfaithful wife of Jehovah. All too frequently the Old Testament in almost brutal clarity reveals Israel's spiritual adultery when that nation embraced the false gods of its neighboring states.

*"They say, If a man put away his wife, and she go from him, and become another man's, shall he return unto her again? Shall not that land be greatly polluted? But thou hast played the harlot with many lovers; yet return again to me, saith the LORD. Turn, O backsliding children, saith the LORD; for I am married unto you, --- Surely, as a wife treacherously departeth from her husband, so have ye dealt treacherously with me, O house of Israel, saith the LORD. (Jer. 3:1, 14, 20).*

Ezekiel chapter sixteen tells in colorful detail Israel's proclivity to wander far from Jehovah God, and the resulting judgmental action taken to bring her back and restore the nation to fellowship. Small wonder that Israel has been placed under the hand of discipline from the LORD as revealed in Ezekiel's prophetic message.

*"But thou didst trust in thine own beauty, and playedst the harlot because of thy renown, and pouredst out thy fornications on every one that passed by; his it was. -- Thou hast committed fornication with the Egyptians, thy neighbors, great of flesh; and hast increased thine harlotries, to provoke me to anger. --*

# Chapter 11

*For thus saith the Lord God: I will even deal with thee as thou hast done, who hast despised the oath in breaking the covenant." (Ezek. 16:15, 26, 59).*

According to God's overall plan, while Israel is being dealt with harshly under correctional judgment, the Lord is busy in His purpose for this age in calling out a body of believers, the Church, from all nations. This body, washed white and clean in the blood of the Lamb (Christ), is referred to as the Bride. In the interval between the failure of Israel under the administration of the law, and the setting up of the Millenial Kingdom at the return of Christ, a Gentile Bride is being called out and established in the place of blessing. This Gentile Bride is none other than the Church. The Bridegroom is the Lord Jesus, as the witness of John the Baptist explains when he makes his claim to be a friend of the Groom. John the Baptist was both kin and close friend of Jesus. In fact, the New Testament reveals that John was a man of some importance in his own right; a man of no small reputation, for it states:

*"This is he of whom it is written, Behold, I send my messenger before thy face, who shall prepare thy way before thee. For I say unto you, Among those that are born of women there is not a greater prophet than John the Baptist; but he that is least in the kingdom of God is greater than he." (Lk. 7:27-28).*

John lived and died before the advent of the Holy Spirit and thus before the Church came into existence. He never was a member of the Church nor ever claimed to be. The passage quoted above says that the least member of the kingdom of God is greater than John. There is only one reason for that to be true but it is a very good reason. The Scriptures say "except a man be born again he cannot see the kingdom of God." (Jn. 3:3). Since the Spirit was not yet on earth in His regenerating ministry, John the Baptist never experienced the "new birth." It is this new birth, the regenerating work of the Holy Spirit, that places a believer in the corporate body of Christ, the Church. The Church had not yet had its beginning in John's day so the Scriptures use the name of the Kingdom of God, which has the same requirement for entrance. John never became a part of the Church, the Bride of Christ. He rightly lays claim to be "friend of the Bridegroom, (which may be the equivalent to the position of "best man" in today's weddings) but he certainly did not know the Bride.

> *"He that hath the bride is the bridegroom; but the friend of the bridegroom, who standeth and heareth him, rejoiceth greatly because of the bridegroom's voice; this my joy, therefore, is fulfilled. (Jn. 3:29).*

In pictures of stark contrast, the Bible compares unfaithful Israel, the adulterous wife of Jehovah, with the Church, the spotless Bride of Christ. Paul, when writing to the believers in Corinth, was elaborating on the good fame of the Bride he said "For I am jealous over you with godly jealousy; for I have espoused you to one husband that I may present you as a chaste virgin to Christ." (II Cor. 11:2).

The words underlined in the above quotation are not found in the Greek of the early manuscripts, but are words added by the translators to give the English version a smoothness of diction and thought. To leave out the two words, you as, is to give the statement a much more positive assertion in declaring the purity of the Bride. What a difference it would make in the Church today if each member could see himself as God sees him in Christ, holy, spotless, sinless, righteous, and wholly acceptable.

The ideal relationship between husband and wife is set forth as being seen in the example of Christ's relationship to the Church. In a rather extended context, Paul embellishes this relationship and it is at this point that he uses that phrase "this is a great mystery."

> *"Husbands, love your wives, even as Christ also loved the church, and gave himself for it, That he might sanctify and cleanse it with the washing of water by the word; That he might present it to himself a glorious church, not having spot, or wrinkle, or any such thing; but that it should be holy and without blemish. So ought men to love their wives as their own bodies. He that loveth his wife loveth himself. For no man ever yet hated his own flesh, but nourisheth and cherisheth it, even as the Lord the church; For we are members of his body, of his flesh, and of his bones. For this cause shall a man leave his*

*father and mother, and shall be joined unto his wife, and they two shall be one flesh. <u>This is a great mystery</u>, but I speak concerning Christ and the church. (Eph. 5:25-32).*

The consummation of this relationship between the Bridegroom and the Bride, the royal wedding, takes place in the heavenlies following the rapture when the Church is caught up to meet the Lord in the air. When this glorious, highly anticipated event occurs, then the believer's salvation will be complete. There are three great benefits that each Christian has yet to obtain - - those benefits that have been deferred to a yet future date - - they will be received and possessed at this time with unsurpassed eternal joy. These three future benefits that will make our salvation full and complete are (1) the release from the sin nature. The old Adamic nature that has caused so much grief and pain will be gone forever; there will no longer be the need to daily reckon it dead. (2) The gaining of heaven itself including heavenly citizenship, and (3) the possession of an immortal, glorious body. Having acquired these three great blessings, our salvation would then be complete; we would be the recipients of all that God has provided for us.

*"Let us be glad and rejoice, and give honor to him, for the marriage of the lamb is come, and his wife hath made herself ready. And to her was granted that she should be arrayed in fine linen, clean and white; for the fine linen is the righteousness of saints." (Rev. 19:7-8).*

This is a royal union that the church enters at this point of her existence. As the Bride of the Son of God, she attains a position of exaltation that could not be reached in any other way. The Church is seated at His side in the role of consort; She reigns with Him. This is the answer to the promise given in the book of Revelation which reads as follows, "And they lived and reigned with Christ a thousand years - - but they shall be priests of God and of Christ, and shall reign with him a thousand years." Rev. 20:4-6. Jesus had given certain promises that believers of the church age would be raised to the heights and the culmination of His intent is recognized in these happenings.

*"And if I go and prepare a place for you, I will come again, and receive you unto myself, that where I am, there ye may be also."* (Jn. 14:3).

*"Father, I will that they also, whom thou hast given me, be with me where I am, that they may behold my glory, - -* (Jn. 17:24).

Christ's own request was that believers might behold His glory, (Jn. 17:24). And the Scriptures verify the results by saying "if so be that we suffer with him, that we may be glorified together." (Ro. 8:17).

## *The High Priest and the Royal Priesthood*

*"Seeing, then, that we have a great high priest, that is passed into the heavens, Jesus, the Son of God, --"* (Heb. 4:14).

*"Now of the things which we have spoken this is the sum: We have such an high priest, who is seated on the right hand of the throne of the Majesty in the heavens, --"* (Heb. 8:1).

*"But ye are a chosen generation, a royal priesthood, -- ."* (I Pet. 2:9).

## *Christ: the Priest Qualifications for the Priesthood*

The work of a priest is to make access to God for men. The Bible says "For every high priest taken from among men is ordained for men in things pertaining to God" (Heb. 5:1). There are five scriptural requirements that must be met before an individual can fill the office of high priest; They are;

1. *He must be a man.* (Heb. 5:1)
2. *He must be called of God.* (Heb. 5:4)

3. He must be washed with water.    (Lev. 8:5-6)

4. He must be anointed with oil.    (Lev. 8:5, 12)

5. He must be thirty years of age.  (Num. 4:3)

If men need priests because sin has separated them from a holy God, and if a blood sacrifice is the only way of acceptance, (Heb. 9:22) then the choosing of an acceptable high priest is of vital interest to men's welfare. Man is solely dependent upon God for instructions concerning the priest's acceptability, for it is the wrath of God that must be placated. Christ was not a member of the tribe or family of Levi from which all the Jewish priests were taken, so He could *not* be after the priestly order of Aaron. Rather, the Scriptures say He was after the order of Melchizedek (Heb. 5:10), a priest of the Most High God (Gen. 14:18).

> *"So also Christ glorified not himself to be made an high priest, but he that said unto him, Thou art my Son, ——— As he saith also in another place, Thou art a priest forever after the order of Melchizedek;" (Heb. 5:5a-6).*

> *"And Melchizedek, king of Salem, brought forth bread and wine; and he was the priest of the most high God." (Gen. 14:18).*

Since the requirements delineated above are for the priesthood in general and not just for the Levitical priesthood alone, they of necessity must apply to Jesus also. We must now look closely through the four gospels to find the fulfillment of these requirements in the life of Christ.

Just before Jesus' public ministry began, John the Baptist was busy in the middle of his ministry baptizing multitudes in the river Jordan. It is to be carefully noted that John the Baptist was a godly man and one who was busy about the work of his Lord. He was of the tribe of Judah and not a Levite, so he did not attempt to intrude in the office of a priest at any point of his ministry. John is said to be a prophet, not a priest, and his ministry centered around the rites of baptism. John abstained entirely from the priestly work of sacrifice at an altar but labored mightily at the river doing the work he was called to do. Jesus appeared there on the bank of the river before John and requested that He too be baptized by John. The Baptist immediately refused Jesus' request for John knew by revelation of the Holy Spirit, the true identity of the man before him; God in the flesh. John's baptism was one "unto repentance" and "of confession of sin" (Matt. 3:2,6,11), and since Jesus, the Son of God, was sinless, He didn't need or require this type of baptism. Nevertheless, Jesus said to John "Suffer it to be so now; for thus it becometh us to fulfill all righteousness" (Matt. 3:15)

The simplest definition of "righteousness" is "doing that which is right". With that definition, it can be understood that Jesus was telling John, though he didn't fully comprehend what was being done, this baptism or washing of water was the right thing, the thing required by the Scriptures to be done. John began to understand the imperative need behind the request, for Matthew continues the narrative by saying, "Then he (John) consented to Him" (Matt. 3:15).

It is plain to see from this account in Matthew's gospel that the event recorded here is not the practice of John's regular baptism, but rather, it is a special occasion following a special request. It is just as plain to see that this is not an example of Christian baptism, for according to Romans 6:3-4, Christian baptism is unto the death, burial, and resurrection of Christ, which events had not yet transpired. Thus we conclude that the baptism of Jesus The Christ was of a special nature, with deep spiritual significance as He prepares to begin His ministry as that of High Priest. One of the requirements was that He be washed with water.

Immediately upon coming up out of the water, "the heavens opened, and the Holy Spirit like a dove descended upon Him" (Mk. 1:10). The Bible uses different illustrations to picture for us the ministry of the Holy Spirit, one such being that of the dove. Another illustration is that of oil, which was used for healing, for comfort, for illumination, and for anointing in specific instances; so the Holy Spirit heals, comforts, illuminates, and consecrates. We recall that one of the requirements for the priesthood was the anointing with oil, which anointing signified the presence and power of the Holy Spirit to be upon the recipient. Thus we perceive the fulfillment of this requirement in Jesus, when the Spirit came upon Him as He emerged from the water following His baptism.

Luke's gospel gives us the key to the age requirement, for though he restricts the story of Jesus' baptism to just two verses (Lk. 3:21-22), his very next statement is that Jesus was about thirty years of age. All five of the listed requirements for entering the office of High Priest and the ministry of making access to God for men were met by Jesus prior to the beginning of His public life. He was a man, both in the sense of being a member of the human race and also in being a male member of that race. He was called of God especially to the office: "The LORD hath sworn, and will not repent, thou art a priest forever, after the order of Melchizedek" (Psa. 110:4; Heb. 5:10). He was thirty years of age when He requested John the Baptist to take Him down into the Jordan river and there submerge Him, washing Him with water. Last of all, we see the Holy Spirit coming upon Him, empowering Him for the work He came to do.

## *The Work of a Priest*

Having now entered into the office of High Priest, His aim or purpose was to make access to God the Father for a fallen, sinful, rebellious race of men. "He became the author of eternal salvation unto all them that obey him" (Heb. 5:9). Part of a priest's duty is to make offerings of "both gifts and sacrifices for sins" (Heb. 9:22). So this High Priest also had to bring a blood offering, if He was to be effective in His ministry.

In the Old Testament economy, worship of God required animal sacrifice. In Leviticus 16:29-34, God prescribed for the nation Israel a day of atonement. On this particularly assigned day, the tenth day of the seventh month, "on that day shall the priest make an atonement for you" (Lev. 16:30). The Old Testament priest was a fallen man like everyone else and needed some provision made for his own sin. Heb. 5:3 God took this into account by establishing the ritual to be followed by the high priest on the Day of Atonement in such fashion that the high priest made atonement for himself before he did so for the people. Lev. 16:6, 11-14, 17. We have already observed that the work of a priest is to make access to God for men; and that is what this passage makes very clear. Sinful men cannot approach a holy God in and for themselves; that requires the mediatorial work of another.

## *Atonement*

Let us pause at this point for a moment and examine the word "atonement". This comes from the Hebrew word "kaphar" which carries as its root meaning "to cover". With this meaning in mind, we see that on the day of atonement the sins of the nation Israel were covered by the blood of an animal sacrifice.

> "And this shall be an everlasting statute unto you, to make an atonement for the children of Israel for ALL their sins <u>once a year</u>" (Lev. 16:34).

What a day this was for that nation. Every Israelite without exception - - man, woman, boy, girl, rich, poor, near, or far -- ALL had their sins of the past year covered on this day.

The emphasis here is on the word atonement (a covering), and the New Testament adds very important light on the subject when it says "For it is not possible that the blood of bulls and of goats should take away sin" (Heb. 10:4). Israel's sin was not removed, it was only covered, and that, year by year as they obeyed God's command and kept this statute. It is for this very reason the doctrine of atonement is confined to the Old Testament and to discussion of the activities of the nation Israel. The word "atonement" is located only once in the New Testament, and that once is confined to the King James or Authorized Version. There, in Ro. 5:11 the word is used as a poor substitute for the more accurate word used in the NASB; reconciliation. In short, atonement is not a New Testament doctrine. Christ's death and shed blood did far more than just cover men's sin. It removed sin -- all sin -- forever. To speak of Christ's death as an atonement is to open wide the door to confusion and error.

Chapter 11

## *Our High Priest*

We have seen Jesus prepared for His role as High Priest; now with that background we will proceed on to see how He filled that role.

*"Neither by the blood of goats and calves, but by his own blood he entered in once into the holy place, having obtained eternal redemption for us." (Heb. 9:12).*

This High Priest, spurning the blood of animals that had been proven ineffective in providing the final and complete solution for sin, brought that which was acceptable: His own blood. "How much more shall the blood of Christ, who through the eternal Spirit offered himself without spot to God" (Heb. 9:14). Having escaped the defilement of Adam's blood through the virgin birth, He was the sinless, spotless Son of God, whose blood was of inestimable value. He was the ONLY answer to the problem of sin.

*"But this man, after he had offered one sacrifice for sins forever, sat down on the right hand of God." (Heb. 10:12).*

*"For by one offering he hath perfected forever them that are sanctified." (Heb. 10:14)*

*"And their sins and iniquities will I remember no more. Now where remission of these is there is no more offering for sin." (Heb. 10:17 - 18).*

This is one of the greatest of all truths for the human mind to grasp and to hold. Jesus Christ's sacrifice of Himself, the offering of His own blood, was not an atonement, not just a covering for sin, but it was a complete removal of sin -- ALL SIN -- for all time and eternity, not one human sin is excepted. On each day of atonement, all the sins of Israel were covered for that one year; on the day that Christ died, all of the sins of the human race were judicially removed forever, including the sins of the past, the present and the future.

Nineteen hundred years ago, Jesus died as a sacrifice for sin, and that included my sin. Obviously I had not been born and had not yet committed any sins, but God in His omniscience had a master plan that was so all-inclusive that it covered me and my generation nineteen centuries after the plan was put into effect. It is an extremely interesting observation that although at this point in my life perhaps half of my sins have become actuality, the remainder are still future, and ALL of them, past and future, are paid for. Jesus, my High Priest, did not just pay the price for past committed sins, but He paid the price for the sins of today and the sins of tomorrow, and the sins of all the tomorrows of the years ahead. How can we help but praise God for "So Great Salvation"!

We see then a great truth. Sin, the cause, and sins, the result, have objectively been dealt with by God, and removed as a condemning and debilitating power; but subjectively sins and iniquities are still factors to be reckoned with in the lives of mortal men.

## *Secure in Christ Jesus*

Having looked at some depth into the subject of "So Great Salvation" and finding this salvation was pre-planned in the councils of God, it was further discovered that the plan is being worked out through the medium of a High Priest, whose duty it is to make access to God for men. The High Priest "called" of God for this significant work, Jesus Christ, proved faithful to His calling and opened the way into the heavenlies, to the very presence of God Himself, for us.

> *"Seeing, then, that we have a great high priest, that is passed into the heavens, Jesus, the Son of God, let us hold fast our profession --- Let us, therefore, come boldly unto the throne of grace, that we may obtain mercy, and find grace to help in time of need." (Heb. 4:14, 16).*

This approach to the Living God in fellowship is just part of the salvation that is being offered as a free gift to any and every man who will simply believe God and reach out to receive it.

> *"For by grace are ye saved through faith; and that not of yourselves, it is the gift of God, not of works, lest any man should boast." (Eph. 2:8-9).*
>
> *"That if thou shalt confess with thy mouth the Lord Jesus, and shalt believe in thine heart that God hath raised him from the dead, thou shalt be saved." (Ro. 10:9).*

For the one who believes and puts his trust in Christ, the High Priest, salvation becomes a present possession and access to God is assured. Because Jesus our High Priest "ever liveth to make intercession" (Heb. 7:25) for us, this access to God will never be broken. God says that we have eternal life -- unbroken face-to-face fellowship with Him -- and that we have passed from death to life, never again to come into condemnation. "And this is life eternal, that they might know thee, the only true God, and Jesus Christ, whom thou hast sent." (Jn. 17:3).

Perhaps the best illustration of this eternal salvation can be seen in a passage of Scripture that is greatly misunderstood by many. Men are totally dependent upon the Spirit of God for enlightenment and subsequent understanding of all truth contained in the Bible. Prayerful and careful heed should be employed in listening to the Spirit while searching out these things.

> *"For it is impossible for those who were once enlightened, and have tasted of the heavenly gift, and were made partakers of the Holy Spirit, and have tasted the good word of God, and the powers of the world to come, if they shall fall away, to renew them again unto repentance, seeing they crucify to themselves the Son of God afresh, and put him to an open shame." (Heb. 6:4-6).*

This Scripture speaks of an impossibility -- the impossibility of a man being saved twice. Those individuals spoken of in this passage are assuredly believers, for the four things they are said to possess are the possessions of every believer. It is stated that they were "once enlightened" -- the light of the gospel shone into their hearts and lives; and that they "tasted the heavenly gift", which free gift of God is salvation. Furthermore it is said "they were made partakers of the Holy Spirit", and when a man possesses the Holy Spirit, it is because the Spirit has taken up residence in his heart, and with Him comes life. Lastly it is said they "tasted the good word of God" -- they knew the truth, they savored the truth, and it became part of them.

> *"But if our gospel be hidden, it is hidden to them that are lost, in whom the god of this world (Satan) hath blinded the minds of them who believe not, lest the light of the glorious gospel of Christ, who is the image of God, should shine unto them."*
> *(II Cor. 4:3-4).*

The men spoken of are saved men; let there be no doubt on this point. It is here that God sets before us a major tenet in the gospel of salvation: if these saved men should ever fall away from salvation, then it is impossible (God's wording) for them to be renewed (saved) again. God is making a positive point.

There is only one way that a believer could possibly be lost, and that is through the failure of his high priest. The work of a high priest is first to make access, and second to maintain that access, to the living God for men. If I am ever lost, it will be because the sacrifice my High Priest, Jesus Christ, brought to God for my redemption was not enough; it was insufficient to do the job. The failure would not be mine, but rather would be that of my High Priest. I have filled all the demands made upon me by God for my salvation. He said, "Believe on the Lord Jesus Christ, and thou shalt be saved". I did believe, and I am saved. It does not take a great deal of perspicacity to see that if my high priest failed and I became lost, it would be impossible for me ever to be saved again. On what grounds could I come? Christ will not die for me a second time, and even though He did, of what value would it be? If His sacrifice of Himself the first time proved to be insufficient, why would the second be any better?

If a man could lose his salvation, to whom could he turn for help? Where could he go? "Neither is there salvation in any other; for there is no other name under heaven given among men, whereby we must be saved." (Acts 4:12).

Chapter 11

# THE INTERCESSOR(S)

*"Wherefore, he is able also to save them to the uttermost that come unto God by him, seeing he ever liveth to make intercession for them." (Heb. 7:25).*

The dictionary defines intercession as 1) "the act of interceding between persons" or 2) "entreaty in behalf of others." *(Reader's Digest Great Encyclopedia Dictionary).*

The plan of salvation that a benevolent God prepared for those who would heed His Word and obey Him, contained two separate intercessors - not one. The Holy Spirit, who is the third person constituting the Godhead, was given as a gift to each believer at the moment of salvation along with the promise He would never leave the recipient. (Jn. 14:16). One of the important ministries His presence denoted was that of intercession. The Word says,

*"Likewise, the Spirit also helpeth our infirmity; for we know not what we should pray for as we ought; but the Spirit himself maketh intercession for us with groanings which cannot be uttered. And he that searcheth the hearts knoweth what is the mind of the Spirit, because he maketh intercession for the saints according to the will of God." (Ro. 8:26-27).*

The Savior Himself is the second of these intercessors. The Lord's work as High Priest did not end with His death and resurrection, but continues in the present with His unceasing intercession for all believers. His intercessory work entails far more than just prayer in behalf of His own. In His role as Shepherd, He leads and guides us around pitfalls and other disasters that only eternity will expose for our recognition, with its resultant outpouring of praise and thanksgiving.

For our enlightenment the Bible actually portrays a court scene with all its attendant characters. The scene is in heaven before the throne where the Father sits as Judge. The prosecutor is Satan who is called "the accuser of the brethren." (Rev. 12:10). It is obvious that "the brethren," you and I, are the defendants; and that we have an Advocate (lawyer) defending us, Jesus Christ the Righteous. (I Jn. 2:1). As often as Satan lays a charge against us because of our sins and iniquities, (he is very busy operating day and night) our Advocate then reminds the court that that sin has been paid for at Calvary and the slate is clean. It is in this manner, through His intercession for us, we are kept in a state where we are totally acceptable to the Father.

This salvation which is in the possession of every believer is perfect for every need and could not be improved upon. On examination we observe that one member of the Godhead, the Holy Spirit, is down here with us taking care of God's interest in His purchased possession on earth; while another member, Jesus Christ, is up there beside the Father taking care of our interests in heaven. Both are interceding for us, and certainly the Father's ear is in tune with what they say.

Like most Christians, I experience those times of great uncertainty when I just don't know how to pray. This happens in all aspects of my prayer life; my personal needs, the local church, my country, the unsaved, missions, and on and on. This corresponds with what the Scripture said in Romans eight quoted above. We do not know how to pray. What a source of comfort and assurance it is to a disturbed heart to know the Spirit is interceding in our behalf according to the will of the Father. The Bible tells us the Spirit abides within each believer and thus He knows and controls the "heart." Because He lives in the heart He knows all the complex issues that pass through that member. God tells us "Keep thy heart with all diligence; for out of it are the issues of life." (Pro. 4:23). Again, His Word says,

> *"A good man, out of the good treasure of his heart, bringeth forth that which is good; and an evil man, out of the evil treasure of his heart, bringeth forth that which is evil; for of the <u>abundance of the heart</u> his mouth speaketh."*

Because of His position, the Spirit is most often aware of our needs before we know we have one. The peace and assurance of the knowledge of His intercession day and night for us in the daily routine of living is just one of the blessings that God so abundantly provides. We are the recipients of "so great salvation."

Chapter 11

Thank God, in His wisdom He appointed His own Son, Jesus Christ the Righteous, to be the High Priest and the Mediator of the plan of salvation; He cannot fail, for He is God.

## *A KINGDOM OF PRIESTS*

Believers are spoken of as a "royal priesthood" (I Pet. 2:9); royal, because they are sons of the Living God, and it is because of this relationship they are heirs of God, joint heirs with Christ. (Ro. 8:17). If that isn't enough, collectively they compose the Church which is "the Bride of Christ" that will one day be seated with Him and reigning as His consort. (II Tim. 2:12; Rev. 20:6). We are a priesthood and we have seen that the work of a priest is to make access to God for men. Believers do not have the duty of making a way for others to approach God; that is the work of Jesus, the High Priest. Our work as a kingdom of priests is to point the way to God, which is to point them to Christ who is "The Way" (Jn. 14:6). Each believer should act as a sign post pointing the way to eternal life. We are witnesses of the resurrected and glorified Lord. It is as faithful men carry out their responsibilities and exercise their spiritual gifts in witnessing of Him, that the Church will continue to grow and the lives of men will be touched and changed.

## Chapter XII

## *The Mystery of the Change Physically: before the rapture*

*"Behold, I show you a mystery: We shall not all sleep, (die) but we shall all be changed." (I Cor. 15:51).*

*"For our citizenship is in heaven, from which also we look for the Savior, the Lord Jesus Christ, who shall change our lowly body, that it may be fashioned like his glorious body, according to the working by which he is able even to subdue all things unto himself." (Phil. 3:20-21).*

God's plan of salvation for His fallen creature, man, is a total plan, complete to the most minute detail, all the way to glory when the regenerated one will be like Christ. This perfect plan is all comprehensive and is designed to include men of all ages past, present, and future. The saints of past ages will be resurrected and will enjoy the presence of and fellowship with their Lord and Savior Jesus Christ; and this they will do in new physical bodies, immortal and incorruptible. But what of living saints, those who at the hour of His coming, are alive and engaged in the tasks of daily living? They are still in their natural, mortal, bodies and thus are not yet fit for dwelling in His presence; an immediate and drastic change is demanded before that euphoric state may be attained. This is precisely the agenda that the Scriptures forecast for the living saint. "We shall not all sleep, (die) but we shall all be changed, in a moment, in the twinkling of an eye." (I Cor. 15:51-52). This change will take place in the physical aspect of man, having to do with the body or more exactly, with the composition or makeup of the body. The Scriptures say "For this corruptible must put on incorruption, and this mortal must put on immortality." (I Cor. 15:53). This truth is further expounded and broadened when the Apostle John says,

> *"Beloved, now are we the sons of God, and it doth not yet appear what we shall be, but we know that, when he shall appear, we shall be like him; for we shall see him as he is." (I Jn. 3:2).*

Like Jesus! What a future is in the offing for the Believer. It is not given in detail what our status shall be in the ages to come, but God has dropped little hints here and there in the post-resurrection activities of His Son, and these glimpses should be enough to raise expectation to high levels of anticipation. One of Jesus' appearances before His disciples after His resurrection is spoken of in the gospel of Luke,

> *"Jesus himself stood in the midst of them, and saith unto them, Peace be unto you. But they were terrified and frightened, and supposed that they had seen a spirit. And he said unto them, Why are ye troubled? And why do thoughts arise in your hearts? Behold my hands and my feet, that is I myself; handle me, and see; for a spirit hath not flesh and bones, as ye see me have. And when he had thus spoken, he showed them his hands and his feet. And while they yet believed not for joy, and wondered, he said unto them, Have ye here anything to eat? And they gave him a piece of a broiled fish, and an honeycomb. And he took it, and did eat before them." (Lk. 24:36-43).*

This passage authenticates the reality of His physical bodily presence, that He was not merely a spirit or ethereal being. There is substance to His form, for He can be touched or handled just like any other man.

It is of equal importance to notice the wording Jesus used in describing Himself when He said "For a spirit hath not flesh and bones, as ye see me have," there being an absence of any mention of blood. Is this omission significant? I believe it is. Resurrection life is on an altogether different principle than that of blood. God created natural man on the principle that the life is in the blood, for He has said, "But flesh with the life thereof, which is the blood thereof, shall ye not eat.: (Gen. 9:4). Pursuing this thought further, at another of His post-resurrection appearances, the Bible says,

## Chapter 12

*"And after eight days, again his disciples were inside, and Thomas with them; then came Jesus, the doors being shut, and stood in the midst, and said, Peace be unto you. Then saith he to Thomas, Reach here thy finger, and behold my hands; and reach here thy hand, and thrust it into my side; and be not faithless, but believing. And Thomas answered --- My Lord and my God. (Jn. 20:26-28).*

In this account, said to be eight days after His resurrection, the open wounds obviously remain in the body of Christ's person. There can be no doubt it is the same body that was bruised and tortured as His enemies vented their anger upon Him; yet it is different, vastly different. These are not scars but are open wounds and no blood; these facts should be as meaningful to the believer of today as they were to Thomas. Christ's blood is still in the ground at the foot of where the cross stood, and it remains forever the price paid for man's redemption from sin. That blood sacrifice Jesus took with Him in His ministry as our High Priest when He ascended on high and sprinkled it in the heavenly sanctuary, thus opening the way to the Father for all who will believe. (Heb. 9:13-14). It is to be understood that His resurrection life is on a completely different principle than that of life prior to His death and resurrection, and this is the same principle being applied in the <u>change</u> that takes place in all living believers at His coming for them.

Concerning the body, the Bible says "it is sown a natural body; it is raised a spiritual body. There is a natural body, and there is a spiritual body." (I Cor. 15:44). The emphasis in this statement is on the physical body, the fact of it's being real, physical, and functional. It is always a body that is placed in a grave, and it is a body that is resurrected from that grave. There is never an account of a body being buried and a spirit subsequently being resurrected. Spirits are not buried in graves; only bodies. The body that comes up from the grave may look the same as the one buried but it is a very different body in its resurrected, glorified state. Most men are somewhat familiar with the functions of the natural body. There is extensive information: knowledge of the circulatory system of the physical body that carries blood to every living cell. In the spiritual body, where life is on another principle than in the blood, there is no need of a circulatory system. There is not the most remote possibility of the glorified body ever receiving a "mortal wound" and bleeding to death.

The respiratory system of the human body is also very familiar, and it is well understood how the lungs transfer life-sustaining oxygen to the blood. This system, too, becomes obsolete and is just so much excess baggage in the spiritual body. This reality is illustrated clearly in the narration of the Lord's ascension into the heavenlies as recorded in Acts, chapter one. As He arose up into the clouds and beyond, there was no apprehension or fear of oxygen starvation leading to strangulation and death. The spiritual body is not restricted by human boundaries nor limited by human needs. The natural bodily functions along with their restrictive systems have no place in the glorious body that God has planned for the saints. The words of John the Apostle take on new significance as he said "It doth not yet appear what we <u>shall be</u> --- but we <u>know</u> that we shall be <u>like him</u>." (I Jn. 3:2).

The resurrection body of the Lord had physical properties unattainable to our present bodies, but will become ours the moment we experience the "change" and gain our bodies of glory. The Lord was able to appear or to disappear at will from closed and locked rooms. His method of movement as well as His speed of movement are sources of amazement and wonder; yet they are properties every Christian will one day possess, for He promised "we shall be like him." One of the attributes of God is the omnipresence of the Holy Spirit; He is everywhere present in the world and in the universe at any given moment. (Psa. 139:5-10). But the Son, Jesus Christ, has limited Himself to a physical body, and thus can only be in one place at one time. This is a limitation imposed upon every physical human being — forever.

With minds focused on this wonderful change that must take place in the physical body to complete salvation in preparation for unlimited, unrestricted fellowship with Him, it is good to give recognition and due praise to the power behind the change. First of all, it is apparent from the Scriptures that this "power" is external to ourselves and comes from without. The Bible says "We shall all <u>BE</u> changed." This conforms with the truth expressed in Hebrews 12:2 where it reads "Looking unto

Jesus, the author and <u>finisher</u> of our faith." Furthermore, this change is instantaneous, "in a moment, in the twinkling of an eye." One moment we are mortal, normal human beings, subject to death, and the next moment we are immortal creatures of eternity. This is not indicative of a slow process worked out or developed over a period of time. Nor is this a condition that the believer strives to obtain or that he evolves into. Rather, it is a condition that is received by an act of God, one that is immediate, irreversible, and eternal. By this act, God has brought the living saint to a par with the resurrected saint, and now both are ready to be "caught up" for fellowship and service in His presence. At this point there is nothing left to delay the "rapture" and the entire Church, "The Bride of Christ" will be caught up into the air, there to be united forever with the Bridegroom.

## Chapter XIII
# *The Mystery of Israel's Blindness*

*"For I would not, brethren, that ye should be ignorant of this mystery, lest ye should be wise in your own conceits: that blindness <u>in part</u> is happened to Israel, <u>until</u> the fullness of the Gentiles be come in. (Ro 11:25).*

Israel nationally turned away from God. Having abandoned their covenant relationship with Him, they turned from the purpose for which He had called them, that of being a witness of the Holy Living God to the pagan and spiritually dark Gentile nations which surrounded them. Instead of converting these Gentile people to the knowledge and worship of the one true God, Jehovah, the people of Israel to a large extent embraced the heathen gods of their neighbors and accepted an idolatrous evil practice. Israel's willing abandonment of God, the God who freed them from years of slavery in Egypt, had its beginnings soon after the death of their great leader, Joshua. Their instructions from Jehovah God included destroying the seven heathen nations that occupied the land of Caanan, Deu. 7:1 and to be a repository of God's word to the rest of the Gentile world. Israel failed miserably in both aspects of that command. The book of Judges gives ample testimony of Israel's failed mission in respect to God's expressed will for them. It was during this time of growing apostasy that the Jewish people first became divided in purpose and in practice. The internal pressures on the nation caused by losing their spiritual stability wrought such intense strife that the nation flew apart. It was only with the establishment of two separate governments under two different kings that the volatile situation began to settle. The two nations, Israel to the north and Judah to the south, never did entirely come to an amicable solution of their differences, and the two engaged in armed combat on a number of occasions. The people continued to forsake God and to neglect spiritual instruction so God, in action clearly designed as discipline, allowed each of the two nations in turn to be defeated and carried into captivity by the very nations they should have been exposing to the light of the one true God.

Because of their continued intransigence, God caused a judicial darkness to fall upon the Jewish people and then instructed the prophet Isaiah to write

> *"And he said, Go, and tell this people, Hear ye indeed, but understand not; and see ye indeed, but perceive not. Make the heart of this people fat, and make their ears heavy, and shut their eyes; lest they see with their eyes, and hear with their ears, and understand with their heart, and be converted, and be healed." (Isa. 6:9-10).*

> *"For the LORD hath poured out upon you the spirit of deep sleep, and hath closed your eyes; the prophets and your rulers, the seers hath he covered. And the vision of all has become unto you like the words of a book that is sealed, --"*
> *(Isa. 29:10-11).*

It was this judicial blindness that caused the leaders of the Jewish people to fail to recognize and ultimately to reject their Messiah Jesus when He came. The spiritual prospects for Israel kept getting less and less with their rejection of Jesus, the Messiah, and their insistence on gaining righteousness by a law. Ro. 9:31

> *"For they, being ignorant of God's righteousness, and going about to establish their own righteousness, have not submitted themselves unto the righteousness of God." (Ro. 10:3).*

As Israel had rejected God, so has He rejected them, not as a nation, or as a people, not even from salvation. God has rejected Israel from occupying the exalted position of privilege, a place in which that tiny nation had exclusive occupancy for centuries. God's rejection of Israel is centered directly on that nation's standing before Him. God dwelt among them, they saw His glory, and they had covenant relationships with Him. Ro. 9:4-5 It was in Jerusalem that the temple (the house of

God) stood; and it was there at the temple where the sacrifices to God were offered and all the activities associated with the Day of Atonement were conducted. Despite these tremendous advantages, Israel never has been a saved nation: nations as such are not "saved"; individuals are. Israel occupied a position of privilege; it was from this lofty position of privilege that Israel fell. In Romans chapter 9, Paul likens this position of privilege (not salvation) to that of an olive tree. The olive tree is not speaking of salvation per-se, but rather it speaks of the "tree of blessing" or even of the "tree of spiritual opportunity." The Jews occupied this place for centuries with the result that there were many godly men among them. But now in the interim they are nationally under the hand of God's judicial chastening, and the Gentiles are being given the opportunity to experience God's forgiveness and blessing. Some, not all, of the natural branches (Israel) are broken off and wild branches (Gentiles) are grafted in. The center of God's attention and activity has been changed from Israel to the calling out of the Church, and that calling is mainly (not exclusively) from the Gentiles. The Gentiles have been elevated to the place of privilege, and many of them are finding salvation.

The judgment of judicial (spiritual) blindness that God placed upon Israel many generations ago is an ongoing judgment that will continue to be so "UNTIL" the Church, "the fullness of the Gentiles" is complete. In a bit of explanation "the fullness of the Gentiles" is speaking of a completed and whole Church body. It began in the book of Acts with the calling out of the Church where it says "Simeon hath declared how God first did visit the nations (Gentiles), to take out of them a people for his name." (Acts 15:14). It is a bit of irony that because Israel failed in its intended ministry to the rest of the world, God laid the nation aside as spiritually blind while He chose another way to reach the Gentile nations.

The "in part" of Israel's spiritual blindness is parallel to the teaching in Romans 11, where the Word says,

> *"And if <u>SOME</u> of the branches be broken off, and thou, being a wild olive tree, were grafted in among them, and with them*

*partakest of the root and fatness of the olive tree,—"*
(Ro. 11:17).

Spiritual blindness to the nation Israel is only "in part" because the Lord is dealing with individuals in this age on a one-to-one basis; the Church is being made up of believers of all nations, <u>both</u> Jew and Gentile. It should be noted that not all the branches of the olive tree were broken off; indeed, the first century church was almost one hundred percent Jewish, Paul himself being an example along with all the disciples of the Lord, with the exception of Judas. The blindness, though national, is not universal to Israel. "Hath God cast away his people?" The inspired answer is "God forbid." (Ro. 11:1).

Soon after the rejection of Jesus as their Messiah (King) and with a growing hostility toward the preaching of His resurrection and His offer of salvation, God saw to it that Israel's whole national system was entirely wrecked, brought to nothing. Using Israel's natural oppressors of that day, the Romans, He had the city of Jerusalem destroyed, and with the destruction of the city the temple was burned; the religious activities and ceremonies that had been established over centuries abruptly ended in the year 70 AD. God couldn't and wouldn't allow the sacrifices and offerings (the types) to continue after Jesus (the Antitype) had been offered once for all. The Bible says

> *"But this man, after he had offered one sacrifice for sins forever, sat down on the right hand of God, —For by one offering he hath perfected forever them that are sanctified. —And their sins and iniquities will I remember no more. Now where remission of these is, there is no more offering for sin.*
> (Heb. 10:12, 14, 17-18).

The Jewish people were subsequently scattered far and wide over the Roman empire.

What had begun as spiritual blindness was now enlarged to spiritual ignorance. No longer having the temple and thus the place to make the offerings and sacrifices, the Jews substituted man-made rituals in their place. The Lord gave warning to the Church to avoid such activity when He said "Having a form of godliness but denying the power of it;

from such turn away." (II Tim. 3:5). Concerning activity in this direction the Scripture goes on to say "even unto this day, when Moses (Old Testament) is read, the veil is upon their (Jewish) heart." (II Cor. 3:15). Many Jews have put to memory large sections of the Old Testament but this word remains head-knowledge only and has never reached their heart to transform their lives. It takes the presence of the Holy Spirit to illumine the Word for heart-understanding. This truth is readily seen in Paul's writing when he said God "hath made us able ministers of the New Testament, not of the letter, but of the spirit; for the letter killeth, but the Spirit giveth life." (II Cor. 3:6).

God has imposed the judgment of spiritual blindness on the nation Israel but He has also restricted the judgment by setting limits to the time it must be endured. The Word says the blindness will prevail "until" a very special event occurs, the completion of the Church, the Bride of Christ. The calling out of the Church and the blindness of Israel are parallel issues. Both will cease during the same event, the second coming of Christ. In the first stage of that event, the Church will be raptured up to meet the Lord in the air; in the second stage, "the Deliverer" will turn away ungodliness from Jacob and "all Israel" shall be saved.

## Chapter XIV
# THE MYSTERY of the SEVEN STARS

*"The <u>mystery</u> of the seven stars which thou sawest in my right hand, and the seven golden lampstands. The seven stars are the angels (messengers) of the seven churches; and the seven lampstands which thou sawest are the seven churches." (Rev. 1:20).*

While banished to the Isle of Patmos, the Apostle John was blessed and encouraged by a visitation from the Lord. It was at this time John received instructions from the Lord to write concerning a specific agenda, for the Lord said,

*"I am Alpha and Omega, the first and the last; and, What thou seest, write in a book, and send it unto the seven churches which are in Asia: -- " (Rev. 1:11).*

The Lord's instructions to John were for him to elaborate on three areas in particular which were given to him in verse nineteen. These areas were:

1) *the things which thou hast seen.* (The vision of the Lord). Chapter 1

2) *the things that are.* (The things that compose the church age). Chapters 2 - 3

3) *the things that shall be hereafter.* (The things that shall occur after the church age). Chapters 4 - 22

The first and third of these areas are quite clear and easily grasped by the reader and do not present a major problem. Chapter one of the book proves to be a short graphic explanation of what John saw as the Lord made Himself known to him. Then the first verse of the fourth chapter states that it is the beginning of the revelation of the things that are to come hereafter. By elimination it may be easily determined that chapters two and three divulge the things that permeate and fill this age in which we live; thus they disclose the things that are. The text verse for this mystery plainly says the seven stars are the angels, or more properly, the messengers of the seven churches chosen from those in Asia Minor. The greater text, that of chapters two and three, show these to be actual churches in seven actual cities in what is now the western part of modern day Turkey: some of the cities are still in existence at this time. John was not only instructed to write to these seven chosen churches, but his instructions included the exact details of that which he was to communicate.

The seven churches of Revelation chapters two and three were not the seven most important congregations in Asia; neither were they the largest, nor were they all churches that the Apostle Paul had founded or visited. Rather they were chosen by the Holy Spirit that they might collectively reveal the course of church history. Each church in its turn was used to represent the condition, the health, and the direction of "Christendom" in consecutive periods of time. The letters to the seven churches reveal church history of two-thousand years to date and give many believers strong impetus for the belief we are living in the final days of the church age and very near the time of the Lord's return. These may be representative churches but it is well to remember they all existed at the same time, and likewise, their counterparts may be found in every generation of the Churches entity.

## *Ephesus Rev. 2:1-7*

The church in Ephesus is historically and spiritually representative of Christendom, all that depicted the church in the world, during the first century. The One who speaks is the sovereign God, and he has somewhat for which to commend this church. His knowledge of them was complete; He knew their works, their sacrificial labors, their patience, and their hatred for Nicolaitanism, the only thing in the New

# Chapter 14

Testament that, it is stated, God hates. Rev. 2:6. Nicolaitanes: the name comes from two words *nikao* which means "to conquer" and *laos* which means "people." It is from the word laos that we get the word "laity" and if the word Nicolaitanes is used here symbolically, it would be in reference to the beginning of a so called priestly order of the clergy which would then divide the church into two groups: clergy and laity, with the former ruling over the latter. It is this uncontrollable lust for religious power and authority that God hates, and it has its roots in the church from the first century. When the Bible speaks of hate, especially the Lord's hate, it is speaking of an inward indignation against evil, against that which is intrinsically wrong. This is not an expression of an evil temper. The message to the church at Ephesus was not that they held the doctrine of Nicolaitanism but that they did not aggressively resist it. That which was hated yet tolerated in Ephesus soon became accepted and practiced in the church represented by Pergamus. This is the message that the churches in America today should hear and heed. Indifference to evil is an insult to a holy God. The sin of the churches is a toleration of evil and of evil men. The Lord said "you have left your first love."

Nicolaitanism reveals a divided church, two divergent camps - clergy and laity - a falsely divided people. God provided for the church to have special gifted men to train other believers to do His will and His work.

> *"And he gave some, apostles; and some, prophets; and some, evangelists; and some, pastors and teachers; For the perfecting of the saints, for the work of the ministry for the edifying of the body of Christ, Till we all come in the unity of the faith, and of the knowledge of the Son of God, unto a perfect man, unto the measure of the stature of the fullness of Christ; --"*
> (Eph. 4:11-13).

In this Scriptural reference there is no provision made for men to sit in judgment or to rule over fellow members. This is the place for the Lord alone. He is the Head of the body, the Church. The Word says to members to "grieve not the Holy Spirit of God" (Eph. 4:30). but does not include grieving men of any caliber in that exhortation. It is this terrible desire in men for power, for authority, to be foremost, that God so hates. In his third general epistle the Apostle John, the same author who wrote concerning Nicolaitanism, directed a few words that have a certain bearing on the subject before us. He wrote,

> *"I wrote unto the church, but Diotrephes, who loveth to have the preeminence among them, receiveth us not. Wherefore, if I come, I will remember his deeds which he doeth, prating against us with malicious words; and not content with that, neither doth he himself receive the brethern, and forbiddeth them that would, and casteth them out of the church."* (III Jn. 9-10).

The message to this church also carries a rebuke; they "left their first love." The speaker did not say they lost their love but rather, they left it. He alone knew this because love is a matter of the heart. Their first burning love for Christ is gone; they were very busy for Him, but He was no longer the center for their affections. Very quickly churchianity had robbed Christ of His place of prominence. This church showed great fervor for service but no great fervor for Him.

The Lord had an exhortation for this church and it consisted of a call back to Himself. First works always follow first love. Along with the exhortation there was issued a warning; unless there was a remembrance of their former position followed by repentance, their lampstand would be removed. History shows that the warning went unheeded and the witness of the church in Ephesus was removed. There is no Christian church in Ephesus today. In fact, there is only a small, mud-hut, rural village where once a large city stood. The city was plundered on numerous occasions by invaders and finally by the Mongols under Tamerlane when it was completely destroyed in 1403 A.D.

## *Smyrna Rev. 2:8-11*

Smyrna contains the word "myrrh" which translates "fragrance" and historically it represents the church of the persecutions that took place in the second and third centuries. The One who speaks to this church is the Eternal God, the great "I AM." Again, as it was at Ephesus,

His knowledge of them is complete. He sees and knows everything about them. He is especially aware of their suffering and martyrdom and, while offering encouragement to be fearless, He leaves with them the promise of a crown of life. There is purpose in suffering and, because of this church's faithfulness, Christianity grew faster and expanded further in this era than at any other time in its existence.

While exhorting this church to be steadfast, He gives them a prophetic message as to the length of the test they face. The Lord's word was they were to be under persecution for ten days; history reveals there were ten major periods of persecution by Roman authority. Reading from Foxe's book of Christian Martyrs, there were ten periods of persecution of the Church by Roman authorities in the first three plus centuries of its existence. These persecutions began in the year 64 A.D. under emperor Nero and it was in this first one that both the Apostles Peter and Paul were slain. Persecutions then continued intermittently during the next two hundred years, the worst two occurring first under the rule of Decius beginning in 249 A.D. and then under Diocletian in 303 A.D. The two mentioned were the 7th and the 10th periods of persecution and were considered to be severe in nature and general in that they touched all parts of the empire. In 323 A.D. Constantine, referred to as the first "Christian Emperor", became ruler and as he ascended the place of power in the empire, he put an end to this long series of martyrdoms. He who permits the test also sets limits beyond which the testing cannot proceed. The church of this period suffered greatly, even unto death, but it was to this same church that the Lord gave the promise they would be free of the second death.

## *Pergamos Rev. 2:12-1*

While the church at Smyrna withstood pressure from without, the church at Pergamos had to face ruin from within. Historically this church represents the period of time when the union between church and state took place, from the fourth to the sixth centuries. Where persecution failed, world conformity succeeded. The marriage of church and state in the early part of the fourth century brought the two together as one with the inevitable result that the state supported and controlled the church.

The Lord describes Himself to those at Pergamos as the One who has the "sharp two-edged sword." In Rev. 19:15 He is reported to have a sharp sword that proceeds out of His mouth, and this sword is symbolic of the Word of God. The Word is a powerful instrument. Moving in one direction, it will save and give life to all who believe it; moving in the opposite direction, it will condemn all who reject Him and His authority as He is revealed by that Word. Because of the illicit union that has taken place, separation is the thing that is lacking in the church of Pergamos; there is a great need for practical sanctification.

The city of Pergamos was the center of the Babylonian cult, and the Christian church there found itself surrounded by a sea of idolatry. Things were in such a state that the Bible sums it up by saying that the city was the site where Satan had his dwelling. Even so, there is reason for commendation for this church. The Lord says concerning them, they "holdest fast my name," and "hast not denied my faith." It was the church of this period that denied the heretical teaching of Arias who disclaimed the deity of Christ and taught that Jesus was only a mortal man. Furthermore, while it is not stated that they did not openly "contend for the faith", neither did they deny it but carried on faithfully in the knowledge that there was salvation in no other but Christ Jesus.

Following the Lord's commendation He went on to show there was also ample reason for rebuke. The Bible says "a little leaven leaveneth the whole lump", and the church of Pergamos was to be no exception. There were those members of the congregation that held to the "doctrine of Balaam", which doctrine led them to abandon their separation and to embrace the practices of the world around them. This opened the door to both idolatry and fornication, and thus personal purity and personal spirituality became a rare commodity among the members of this church. Security in Christ is not a license to sin and to participate in worldliness or to engage in sins of the flesh.

A second area for rebuke opened when the church made the decision to accept the doctrine of the Nicolaitanes. That which was hated and avoided by the first century church [Ephesus] had been accepted as doctrine and put into practice by this fourth century church. The laity thus became subservient to an entrenched clerical hierarchy. The sin of the church was the toleration of evil, especially evil, unsaved leaders as members of the clergy.

The double rebuke was followed by a dire warning: "I will fight against them". The weapon to be used was the sword of His mouth which is the Word of God. It is a fearful thing to have the Living God in open opposition to one's stand, but to have this occur to a major portion of the recognized church on earth is almost beyond credence. In every generation and through all circumstances God has His faithful remnant and He gives His recognition to this group found in Pergamos. It is to the overcomer that the promise is given that they would eat of the "hidden manna" which once again is reference to the Word of God, the Bible. This is the source that assures the believer, "The just shall live by faith" (Heb. 10:38), and that "faith cometh by hearing and hearing by the Word of God" (Rom. 10:17)

## *Thyatira Rev. 2:19-29*

Historically Thyatira represents the church of the sixth through the fifteenth centuries which is the age of the papacy. The name Thyatira is translated by some to mean "continual sacrifice" which would mean the *"mass"*, and the mass is the very heart of Roman Catholicism. The mass denies the finished work of Christ and inevitably led to the dark ages and to medieval Christianity. This is the full blown fruit of Nicolaitanism.

The One who speaks to this church is the Son of God. What a contrast, for to the Roman church He is only the son of Mary. The text says He has "Eyes like a flame of fire". He sees everything; nothing is hidden from Him. He also has "feet like fine brass;" and as brass typifies judgment, this One will not tolerate or close His eyes to evil. He is the omniscient God; He knows all. It is repeated twice that He knows their works, and He indicates their works are more prominent than their faith or their love.

*Mysteries of the New Testament*

The Lord finds it necessary to give this church a very strong rebuke, for He said He had a "few things against" them. First He brings before them the name Jezebel, the woman who led Israel into idolatry and immorality. The inference was that those in Thyatira were walking the same ungodly path. Jesus then says He gave them space or time to repent and they did not; it may be well to recognize that the Lord dealt with this church for a full millenium. The Word of God was no longer this church's authority, but the word of the organized church had taken His place. The professing church was being led away from the person of Christ into a man-devised system, from Christ to Mary and from the cross to the mass.

Judgment takes a prominent place in the Lord's address to the church of Thyatira and brings the first mention of great tribulation. Her children are spoken of in verse 23 and it can be readily understood that Protestantism came out of Roman Catholicism and brought with it many of the evils of the parent organization. The lack of Spiritual unity and the propensity toward division seen in the continual splintering into more and more denominations certainly is not of God. Yet all is not lost; the Lord says, "But that which ye have already, hold fast till I come." His appeal is to those who are separate from the mass of profession — true born again believers. One of the sources of encouragement is seen in the promise given to the "overcomer" in each of the churches, or in each represented age. To the overcomer of Thyatira Jesus promises "power over the nations", this being connected to His second coming and the establishment of the Millennial Kingdom when Church saints will rule and reign with Him. The irony to be detected in this promise is that power or control over the nations is exactly what the papacy has been striving for over the centuries.

Another truth that gives the believer a sobering look at reality is that Jesus said to this church, "Hold fast till I come." In His previous messages the thrust was to return to a former state in their relationship with the Savior. His key words were remember, repent, and return. Now He indicates the only hope for the church is in His coming back to be personally present with them. The condition of the church, as seen when afflicted with the burden of the papacy, has gone beyond the point of no return. They received His promise that He would put no further burden upon them; they had all they could bear. The only escape now from an intolerable situation lay in the promise of His soon return.

## *Sardis Rev. 3:1-6*

Sardis means "a remnant" and historically it represents the church of the fifteenth through the seventeenth centuries and is known as the church of the Reformation. This church period resulted as a strong backlash to the conditions existing under Thyatira, the church of the papacy. That a change was desirable, even mandatory, is widely recognized, for the church in general had gradually declined away from God until "true faith" could hardly be found. Action in the Church is commendable, for the Church is instructed to go, to pray, to make disciples, over all to witness to the power of the resurrected Lord. On the other side of the equation, reaction to an existing situation is almost always detrimental and the church of Sardis represents reaction at its worst.

The One who speaks to this church at Sardis is the same who has the sevenfold Spirit of God, signifying He is the all sufficient One. He is able to meet their every need; there is no room nor necessity for mariolatry if they would only allow Him to occupy His rightful place as Head of the Church. He holds the seven stars which represent the testimony of the Church. Apart from Him all ministry of the church is dead works. The Lord carries a dreadful announcement to this church when He summarizes "I know thy works, that thou hast a name that thou livest, and art dead." That is a terrible indictment, but it reveals the lack of Spirituality in the work of the Reformation as a whole.

Protestantism arose bearing strong protest against error and corruption, but the protest became diluted by failure to put Jesus Christ in His rightful place as Head of the Church. When He is given that place, there is found no place for spiritual vacuum nor for intrusion by men. The thing that is said the Lord hated, Nicolaitanism, has been allowed to continue, and its presence is seen in the establishment of various state churches. This carried-over error made it possible for individuals to be declared members of the church because of their physical birthright or their citizenship rather than by regeneration, being born again.

"Thou hast a name that thou livest, and art dead." The Scriptures do not say this is a dying church but one that was spiritually lifeless. The Protestant reformation brought on lifeless profession—dead orthodoxy. Men preferred to be doctrinally correct but Spiritually bankrupt; as Paul wrote to Timothy, "Having a form of Godliness, but denying the power of it; from such turn away." (II Tim. 3:5). The battle cry of the Reformation was "justification by faith alone" but that has long since been lost to the greater part of Christendom. Leader competed with leader over doctrinal issues and Protestantism splintered and fractured until it was virtually unrecognizable. At best it may be said that the Reformation began well, but it quickly deteriorated into a series of religious systems that the Lord has described as being spiritually dead—lifeless.

## *Philadelphia*

In all the record of church history the message to the church at Philadelphia alone carries a definite note of praise and has no rebuke of any kind. Philadelphia is a combination of two Greek words, "phileos" and "delphia" meaning brotherly love. Philadelphia is the church that historically represents Christendom in the eighteenth through the twentieth centuries, the church of the "open door" especially as it refers to the mission field. The faithful remnant of Sardis has developed into the equally faithful church of Philadelphia while the remainder, those that comprised the dead profession that is so abhorrent to the Lord, developed into the church of Laodicea. In contrast, the church of Smyrna became known as the suffering church having to withstand persecution from without, the source being the pagan world. The church of Philadelphia is known as the weak church, its conflict coming from within, the source being the religious world.

The One who speaks to the church at Philadelphia is the omnipotent, all-powerful, sovereign God, who as to character is holy, One to be trusted, having complete authority. To this church, one declared to have but little strength, He has given an "open door" that no man can shut, a missions opportunity par excellence, never again to be equalled. His praise of the Philadelphia church is liberal and extends into a number of areas in which they have excelled. These areas include: 1) they were weak but not totally without strength, and they were not afraid to use what they had, 2) they kept His Word and gave it its proper place as the final basis of authority, 3) they kept the Word of His patience, making His return a reality in their daily living as well as in their doctrine, and 4) they did not deny His name but made Christ the center of their lives.

The church age represented by Philadelphia is unique above all others in that it is the one that received promise of escape from the time of trial (tribulation) that is due to come on all earth dwellers. To this church alone He said, "Behold, I come quickly," signifying His return is imminent.

## *Laodicea Rev. 3:14-22*

Laodecia: the church of the last days — the seventh and last of those assemblies chosen to portray the history of the church on earth. Historically, it represents the church of the twentieth (and twenty first?) century. The name Laodecia itself tells a story. Made of a combination of two words, "laos" and "dicea", it translates into the "people speak" or the "people rule." The plans and goals of this church are made to satisfy the people — not Christ. The voice of the people is the final authority instead of the word of God. This is democracy in full flower; it may be workable in politics, or in society, even in business and commerce, but it is death in the church. The message to the church of Philadelphia contained no rebuke; the message to the church of Laodicea contains no praise.

The One who speaks refers to Himself as "the Amen" whose words are the final testimony revealing Divine certainty. He is "the faithful and true witness" emphasizing that His is an absolutely true report. The speaker to each church is Christ, and He describes Himself to each church in terms as befitting the needs of the church being addressed. As in the case of each of the former churches, to this one also, He acknowledges He knows their spiritual condition. He calls them lukewarm — neither hot nor cold — but neutral, showing only indifference to Christ. They boast of their riches, of their independence — they have no need, of anything or of anybody. This church boasts of everything but ignorance; but the Lord assesses their condition by saying they know not their true condition which is wretched, poor, blind, and naked. Because of their wretched condition which they refuse to recognize, the Lord says of Laodicea that He would cast them out; they disassociated themselves from Christ; He in turn refuses to recognize them as His own. Philadelphia had the Lord's promise to be delivered from trial, to be "caught up" while Laodicea received the awful warning that they are to be "spewed out" of His mouth as being a distasteful, detestable object.

The Lord proceeds to address the needs exposed at Laodecia by saying they should "buy gold tried in the fire." Gold speaks of that which has intrinsic value, is unadulterated or is spiritual and heavenly. Secondly, He expresses their need to buy white raiment to cover their nakedness, the white raiment representing righteousness. He followed by saying this church was blind and counseled them to buy eye salve. With eyes anointed they might receive spiritual light which was one of their most desperate needs. His call to Laodecia is to individual fellowship, and regardless of the overall condition of the church, the Lord <u>always</u> has a faithful few. To these, the overcomers, He promises the right to sit with Him on His throne. This promise intimates close association with Christ in His kingdom which is soon to follow.

The sequence of the Lord in His relationship to these churches is something to note. To Sardis He said, "hold fast till I come;" to Philadelphia He said, "Behold I come quickly;" and to Laodecia His words were "Behold, I stand at the door." There is no further reference or message to a church after that which is directed to Laodecia. This fact stands as a bit of evidence that Laodecia is truly the church of the last days of the age.

## Chapter XV
# *MYSTERY BABYLON*

*"And upon her forehead was a name written, MYSTERY, BABYLON THE GREAT, THE MOTHER OF HARLOTS AND ABOMINATION OF THE EARTH." (Rev. 17:5).*

Revelation chapter seventeen is the greater context from which the text verse is taken. The entire chapter is given over to the identity, description, and destruction of an extremely unsavory, ungodly character named "the great harlot." The opening verses read as follows:

*"Come hither; I will show unto thee the judgment of the great harlot that sitteth upon many waters; With whom the kings of the earth have committed fornication, and the inhabitants of the earth have been made drunk with the wine of her fornication." (Rev. 17:1-2)*

The great harlot is an expressive and vivid description of religious defection and of spiritual uncleanness that follows the removal of the Holy Spirit along with the True Church from the earth. This description fits the false church which is composed of everything religious left behind on earth when the true Church is raptured away. The true Church is called the spotless, pure, virgin bride of Christ; what a contrast this makes to the woman being described here. The great harlot is the consummation of the spiritual deficiency that was seen in the church of Laodecia of which the Lord said "I will spew you out." "However, the great harlot is not confined to this group only, but is an amalgamation of all false religions world wide. This is ecumenical ecclesiasticism at its zenith — a truly world religion — but one without Christ.

*Mysteries of the New Testament*

The true Church is a New Testament mystery in that it was entirely unknown to the Old Testament. The false church, mystery Babylon, is also a New Testament mystery in that it was not revealed until the Lord spoke to the Apostle John and commanded him to write that which is now found in the book of Revelation. The Apostle Paul had written earlier concerning "the mystery of iniquity" as seen in a previous chapter, (X) and now it can be readily observed that the false church is the antithesis of the true church, which is the virgin bride of Christ, and the false church is utterly filthy, degraded, the consummation of the working of the mystery of iniquity.

When first seen, the great harlot is astride and riding a scarlet colored beast, (Rev. 17:7). This beast is said to be representative of masses of people — great multitudes. This proves to be the same beast described in some detail in Daniel chapter seven verses nineteen through twenty eight and is thought by many to represent the restored Roman empire. To be astride and riding the beast would indicate the harlot had the beast under her control and was actually determining in which direction and at what speed she wished the beast to go. Furthermore, Revelation 17:18 relates the harlot to a great city, most probably Rome, which city rules, and has ruled, over many kings here on earth. The Vatican in Rome has been the religious authority that has directed the destiny of nations for centuries. One of the major claims of Rome was that it had authority over all civil power. In approximately the year 860 A.D. Pope Nicholas I formulated the medieval idea of the papacy and carried out the papal claim to world supremacy. In the centuries following, Rome has done its best to enforce or even augment this claim. This bestial empire is seen flourishing in full power and authority under the auspices of the Antichrist in the last days until the time of the Lord's second advent and the installation of the Messianic kingdom.

The Babylonian harlot is named the "Mother of harlots" and, as such, is the fountainhead of all false religion. Idolatry, the worship of false gods, began at Babylon under that arch-apostate Nimrod, the grandson of Ham, who was the son of Noah as told in Genesis chapter eleven. It is of passing interest to note there is no recorded instance of idolatry prior to the flood. Godlessness, yes; self-righteousness, yes; paganism, yes; but idolatry — the worship of something other than the Living God — no. Idolatry began at Babylon and is Babylonian from that time until this present day and will continue to be so until its most tragic and bitter end recorded in the Book of Revelation. The worship of false gods, or pseudo-religion, has been a curse on mankind ever since. The Babylonian harlot is clothed in raiment that outwardly imitates that which the true Church is inwardly. The true Church is the habitation of the Living God (Eph. 2:19-22), and because God dwells within, she is beautiful inwardly and spiritually.

> *"Now, therefore, ye are no more strangers and sojourners, but fellow citizens with the saints, and of the household of God; And are built upon the foundation of the apostles and prophets, Jesus Christ himself being the chief corner stone, In whom all the building fitly framed together groweth unto an holy temple in the Lord; In whom ye also are built together for an habitation of God through the Spirit." (Eph. 2:19-22).*

God has said "Be ye holy for I am holy"; to be holy means to be pure, clean, chaste, and unspotted. The harlot outwardly before the world looks good to the eye, for she is clothed in that which is deceptive. The attire of the harlot is wonderfully imitative. The Saints are said to be dressed in white raiment which is typical of righteousness. (Rev. 19:8). In contrast to that the harlot is clothed in colors of purple and scarlet. Purple is the color of royalty and rightly belongs to the true Church which is the espoused bride of Christ, the King of kings. Scarlet is the color of both redemption and life — these are possessions of the saved, the true Church. The harlot has no sign of righteousness on her vesture, but in reality she has all the imitative signs of the Old Testament service in the tabernacle and under law, which service was done away.

The tabernacle of old was the dwelling place of God among the people of Israel. "And let them make me a sanctuary, that I may dwell among them." (Ex. 25:8). It is described in the Old Testament as having this same color arrangement and was extremely beautiful on the inside.

> *"Moreover thou shalt make the tabernacle with ten curtains of fine-twined linen, and blue, and purple, and scarlet; with cherubim of skillful work shalt thou make them." (Ex. 26:1).*

Outwardly the tabernacle was very plain and unassuming. Its outside covering was a blanket made of badger skins that may be thought of as a light, leather, weather-proof sheet. There was nothing attractive about the tabernacle in its outward appearance; one had to enter in order to see the beauty.

The Babylonian harlot has all the accoutrements to skillfully imitate the true Church; yet inside, she is filthy and unchaste. The Bible says that she is a drunken murderer.

> *"And I saw the woman drunk with the blood of the saints, and with the blood of the martyrs of Jesus; and when I saw her, I wondered with great wonder." (Rev. 17:6)*

The colors and symbolism we see associated with the beast and the harlot were very prominent in the tabernacle setting. The curtains and veils inside the tabernacle were fitting adornment for the presence of the Living God. It is here where one first sees the purple and blue and scarlet and the fine-twined linen with the cunningly woven cherubim throughout. A truly fitting setting for our God, every detail revealing some glorious phase of His magnificent holy character. I believe with the Shekinah Glory in the Holy of Holies behind the inner veil, the veil must have just shimmered with beauty and the woven cherubim would have appeared to have taken on a life of their own. This is the scene that Satan would attempt to imitate — and while he could make a fairly good facsimile on the outside, working with the accoutrements of the harlot — on the inside she remained vile, filthy, and full of abominations.

In the book of Revelation Chapter 13 is recorded and revealed two different men who are referred to as being beasts. This designation is given to them because of both their character and their conduct. The unspeakable crimes against mankind they are said to commit, result in untold misery, destruction, and death for men on earth. These men are leaders during the time of "tribulation". The first mentioned becomes the civil leader over all the earth; the second is the religious leader or authority. The two appear on the world scene only after the True Church has been raptured into heaven and is found there enjoying the presence of the Living God who saved them. Both of the men, referred to as beasts, are in places of great authority and they are tools of Satan, sold out to him.

The second "beast" is described as having two horns like a lamb, but when he opens his mouth to speak, he speaks as the dragon. (Rev. 13:11). Using any words, could there be a more apt description of a man having the spirit of antichrist? Outwardly he appears meek and mild like a lamb, but his spoken ideas and interests are definitely contrary to the revealed will of God. This is the man who is in control of worship and is able to perform seeming miracles to deceive those who remain on earth. He is the one who is the leader, the heart and soul, the head of "Mystery Babylon", the false church. He is the one who causes all the world to worship an idol that is made in the image of the civil leader, the first beast. Going a step further, he also demands that all men receive a certain mark without which they can neither buy nor sell. This second beast of Revelation 13 is known elsewhere in Revelation as the False Prophet. (Rev. 19:20). In the role of False Prophet, he is the individual who is the chief architect in constructing the evil complex system that brought "Mystery Babylon", the great harlot, to the crest of popularity and power. Along with his contemporary, the civil leader, and also with Satan the patron of both men, they compose the trinity of evil.

The dressed up harlot, the false church, urged on by its leader, is very instrumental in getting the first beast, the civil authority, into the seat of highest power and authority here on earth. It is simply a case that once again the civil and religious authorities work together in collusion to gain a common goal. Once that goal is attained, at least as far as the civil leader being ensconced in the seat of power, it is seen he (the civil leader) can tolerate no possible rival to his authority, so he turns on the harlot and has her utterly destroyed. This peak of evil nearly reaches the point of incredibility. Apparently the civil authority is not only anti-god but is also antireligious. He sees to the destruction of the base of operations of his potential rival, the one who aided him in attaining his seat of power. It is in this manner that organized religion on earth comes to its end, and that at the hands of the government in power.

> *"And the ten horns which thou sawest upon the beast, these shall hate the harlot, and shall make her desolate and naked, and shall eat her flesh, and burn her with fire. For God hath put in their hearts to fulfill his will, and to agree, and give their kingdom unto the beast, until the words of God shall be fulfilled." (Rev. 17:16-17).*

> *"How much she hath glorified herself, and lived luxuriously, so much torment and sorrow give her; for she saith in her heart, I sit a queen, and am no widow, and shall see no sorrow. Therefore shall her plagues come in one day, death, and mourning, and famine, and she shall be utterly burned with fire; for strong is the Lord God who judgeth her. And the kings of the earth, who have committed fornication and lived luxuriously with her, shall bewail her, and lament for her, when they shall see the smoke of her burning, Standing afar off for fear of her torment, saying, Alas, alas, that mighty city! For in one hour is thy judgment come." (Rev. 18:7-10).*

This, then, is the end to which all false religion is heading. The great harlot, the false church, was manipulated by the trinity of evil and all three of these individuals suffer the same fate when the One True God, whose power, place, and authority they attempted to usurp casts them into the lake of fire. (Rev. 20:10) There they will be in torment forever.

One cannot say God has not given ample warning of judgment to come. The gospel still goes out to needy men, and God is still saying "—behold, now is the accepted time; now is the day of salvation". (II Cor. 6:2b).

## Chapter XVI

## *THE MYSTERY OF GOD IS FINISHED*

*"But in the days of the voice of the seventh angel, when he shall begin to sound, <u>the mystery of God should be finished,</u> as he hath declared to his servants, the prophets. (Rev. 10:7).*

This study began with the posit that the church age is the "mystery age." All of the "New Testament Mysteries" were relevant and valid only to the Church on earth. The so called "mysteries" were unknown prior to the introduction of the Church. Then, as has been shown in this study, they were revealed one by one to the growing number of believers in the infant Church of the early days of this present age to expose them to the greatness of their calling. No other people in history has the opportunity to walk in union and closeness of fellowship with God as do the believers of this the church age. We, of all people, have been signally blessed as we have been made the "righteousness of God in him." (II Cor. 5:21).

These blessings have been stated in a rather positive fashion in this study because of the "great and precious promises" God has given to us. We have no desire to appear overly dogmatic on the subject of the mysteries but we do want to teach with the utmost confidence and alacrity where God has spoken. We are told on many occasions and with different words that through the aid of the Holy Spirit we would <u>know</u> these precious truths. Typical of God's promise is that which is written in the first chapter of the book of Ephesians.

*"That the God of our Lord Jesus Christ, the Father of glory, may give unto you the spirit of wisdom and revelation in the knowledge of him, the eyes of your understanding being enlightened; that ye may know what is the hope of his calling,*

*and what the riches of the glory of his inheritance in the saints, —." (Eph. 1:17-18).*

The remaining verses of that chapter (19-23) are equally illuminating as to assurance and confidence in the blessings God has promised to those who believe. We may retain a spirit of boldness in our teaching touching on the subject of the mysteries because God has spoken; and with the spoken word we have the Spirit living within us with the promise from the Father that He (the Spirit) will teach us all things concerning the truth. Further He said "And you shall know the truth, and the truth shall set you free." (Jn. 8:32).

*"And I will pray the Father, and he shall give you another Comforter, that he may abide with you forever; even the Spirit of truth, whom the world cannot receive, because it seeth him not, neither knoweth him: but ye know him; for he dwelleth with you, and shall be in you. — But the Comforter, who is the Holy Spirit, whom the Father will send in my name, he shall teach you all things, and bring all things to your remembrance, whatever I have said unto you." (Jn. 14:16-17, 26).*

It is because of His love for us that God first provided and then revealed the depth of the riches that are found in the study of the New Testament mysteries for those who are willing to dig a little. All the vital statistics of the Church are made known through a study of this nature. The Lord shows us the beginning, the character, the message, the course, the relationship with Christ, the destiny, and the glory of the Church. All these truths and more, are seen in the Church prior to its completion and its home going as displayed in the New Testament. The Church is brought to its terminus on earth and is raptured away. The fullness of the Gentiles has been brought in and the mystery age comes to an end. There are no further mysteries of the Church to be revealed; the Church is complete, perfect, glorified, and seated next to the Bridegroom in the heavens.

The text quoted at the beginning of this chapter is taken from Revelation chapter ten and is referring to the time in God's plan when the True Church has already been raptured from the earth and the corrupt church which has been left behind, (mystery Babylon) has been destroyed. There is no vestige of the church of any sort left here on earth. Any and all source of restraint has been removed. Anarchy reigns. The blowing of the trumpet by the seventh angel proclaims the final and closing events of the "great tribulation" period on earth. It is during the sounding of this seventh trumpet that the seven bowls of wrath are poured out on mankind. It is said that unless this period of time was reduced in its magnitude no flesh would survive.

> *"For then shall be great tribulation, such as was not since the beginning of the world to this time, no, nor ever shall be. And except those days should be shortened, there should no flesh be saved; —"* *(Matt. 24:21-22).*

This time of purging is absolutely necessary and required for the sake of righteousness and justice but God, who is both loving and merciful, has limited the time of wrath and judgment. Immediately following this unprecedented period of wrath, the Lord appears on earth for the second time. His physical presence being a reality, the millenial kingdom will then be established and all Church Saints, who have returned with the Lord, will also be present. These Church Saints will be in a fixed state of being, for the Bible says of them:

> *"So, when this corruptible shall have put on incorruption, and this mortal shall have put on immortality, then shall be brought to pass the saying that is written, Death is swallowed up in victory."* *(I Cor. 15:54).*

This is one of the great focal points in the history of the Church. This is the beginning of that time when the Church Saints have been chosen to rule and reign with Christ. There is no longer need for the "mysteries" and God says let them be finished.